Praise for *The Money Puzzle*

"Austin Cheviron's *The Money Puzzle* transforms complex financial concepts into a clear, actionable roadmap for wealth creation. Through authentic storytelling and practical systems. Austin doesn't just inspire you to dream about financial freedom—he equips you with the exact tools to achieve it."

Glenn Sanford,
Founder, CEO, and Chairman
of the Board, eXp World Holdings, Inc.

"Austin Chevron's story is one of the most compelling I've seen. It's not just a rags-to-riches story; it's how fast he turned his life around. In just a few years, he went from rock bottom to a seven-figure net worth. Most books by coaches are just teasers for a coaching program, but in Chapter 13, he lays it all out plainly. No fluff, no upsell. I've heard him speak on these principles, and what I respect most is how he simplifies the path to wealth. It's clear, actionable, and it works. I highly recommend this read."

Remington Ramsey,
Creator of Real Producers and Best-Selling Author

"Austin Cheviron has done a brilliant job breaking down what can often feel overwhelming into clear, simple, and actionable steps. This book gives you the foundation every family needs to build wealth from shifting your money mindset to protecting what matters most and intentionally growing your income and investments."

Jairek Robbins,
Founder of Performance Coach
University, Author, Investor

"I've known Austin my entire life, and there's truly no one better to learn from about money. He is the perfect blend of Dave Ramsey's discipline and Robert Kiyosaki's wealth-building mindset. His approach is practical, powerful, and proven."

Nate Cheviron,
Co-Founder of Cheviron Coaching

"Achieving financial success can be puzzling. It's our obligation as we grow to seek out resources to help us prosper. *The Money Puzzle* is designed to help us put the pieces together to gain control of our relationship with money. Its timing couldn't be better for showing us how to get our financial feet on the ground."

Tom Hopkins,
Author of *How to Master the Art of Selling*

THE MONEY PUZZLE

A Family's Guide to Putting the Financial Pieces in Place

THE MONEY PUZZLE

A Family's Guide to Putting the Financial Pieces in Place

AUSTIN CHEVIRON

MADE FOR SUCCESS

Made for Success Publishing
www.MadeForSuccess.com

Distributed by Blackstone Publishing

First Printing

Library of Congress Cataloging-in-Publication data
Author Cheviron, Austin
The Money Puzzle: A Family's Guide to Putting the Financial Pieces in Place
p. cm.

LCCN: 2025943982
ISBN: 978-1-64146-957-9 *(Hardcover)*
ISBN: 978-1-64146-958-6 *(eBook)*
ISBN: 978-1-64146-959-3 *(Audio)*

Printed in the United States of America

For further information, contact Made for Success Publishing
+1(425)526-6480 or email service@madeforsuccess.net

To my children.
May this book guide you to the wealthy life you deserve.
Let my failures that you never saw be the wisdom
you pass down to your children.
I love you both,
Dad

CONTENTS

FOREWORD
by Tom Hopkins

WE ALL HAVE dreams for our lives—dreams of the type of homes we will live in, the cars we will drive, and vacations we might share with loved ones. We educate ourselves, developing the skills to earn the income that will support our dream and that lifestyle. We then work hard to earn the money to attain the dream.

Becoming successful in our careers is usually a pretty clear path. This can make earning money pretty easy when we just follow the path. Making the most of the money we earn requires an entirely different set of skills.

Understanding money, how it works, and how it can work for us is a whole educational curriculum. However, without the knowledge and discipline to apply that education, many find themselves adrift, unable to explain where their money goes. We never seem to have enough.

In *The Money Puzzle*, Austin Cheviron shares easy-to-follow instructions for analyzing our current financial situations, not just the money itself, but also how we think about it and why. With a better understanding of how to relate to and manage money, we can take advantage of the many strategies he lays out for building a solid foundation to achieve our lifestyle goals and the legacy we leave behind. By gaining more control over your money, you reduce the amount of financial stress in your life. That alone makes reading this book worthwhile!

As someone who has spent decades training more than five million sales professionals worldwide and authoring bestselling books on success, I've seen what works and what doesn't when it comes to building a prosperous life. I found it interesting that Austin's career path has been similar to my own. We both got our start in real estate. We both learned by watching others around us either succeed or fail with the money they acquired. We are both always seeking better ways of accomplishing our dreams. And we are both dedicated to sharing the knowledge we gain with others—to make their paths smoother.

I greatly admire the work Austin has put into simplifying the steps to take you from financial confusion and anxiety to having a firm handle on your money, making it work harder for you than you do to earn it. Austin has proven that he lives what he teaches. He's not just writing from theory. He made the same mistakes we all do. He figured out a better way. And even today, as he continues to walk the path, he mentors others with real results.

I highly recommend using this book as a toolkit. Read it, of course, but also do the work Austin has laid out. It will take a time commitment that I believe is well worth it to gain a clearer understanding of why you relate to money the way you do, where it's all going, and simple steps to improve your financial future. Start putting the pieces of your money puzzle together. You will be pleasantly surprised by how your life changes for the better, allowing you to build a better future. Don't just dream of wealth, build it. Let this book be your blueprint.

Tom Hopkins
Best-selling author,
How to Master the Art of Selling

INTRODUCTION

GROWING UP, MY family's financial state wasn't great, but it wasn't awful either. As an upper lower-class family, my dad didn't share with me the times he struggled, the days he scraped enough change together to buy milk for us.

I was seven when my parents divorced. Every other Friday felt like Christmas at my mother's home. It was payday, which meant one thing: we were going grocery shopping! Her paycheck wasn't much, but it was enough to cover the essentials and leave just a little room for something extra for each of us.

I remember the two things my mom always treated herself to: a case of Diet Coke and a case of Bud Light. The Bud Light, in particular, is a very clear childhood memory of mine because I was often the one tasked with cleaning up the Bud Light mess on Saturday morning. What mess, you ask? The one in the freezer. You might wonder why she kept her beer in the freezer. Simple. Buying it warm saved us 60 cents at the store.

She was great at making things fun for us. When we lived in a one-bedroom house, she created a bedroom for my sister and me out of a tiny closet with a bunk bed and a sheet for a door. We would joke about "closing the sheet" as if it were a door when it was time to get up and get going.

Though we didn't have a lot, we always had a place to live and food on the table. When you're a kid, that's all that matters, isn't it? We weren't financially rich by any means. However, we were rich in love. I never felt any insecurity in the relationships I had with my loved ones.

One very important message I received from Grandma Clem, my father's mother, was that any money I received was mine, and that I should be a good steward of it. She taught me well. I earned money doing chores and helping neighbors, and I also received some as gifts for birthdays and Christmas. I had a savings account and got great satisfaction watching that bank account grow.

Today, I may not be in the top 10 percent of people who can show you how to earn more money. However, I would happily go up against the top 2 percent of people in the world for wise money management. After all, the real secret to wealth is making your money work for you so you can do what you really want in life.

Initially, I set out to write the stories and strategies that helped create my wealth for my kids. Because of my efforts, my kids won't grow up with many financial hardships. While this is a blessing, it's also a two-edged sword; they enjoy the blessing of having a comfortable life. But there is also the downside of not learning the lessons that financial challenges bring. They won't learn, the hard way, about effective strategies for handling money. They won't struggle financially unless they really go out of their way to mess things up, and that doesn't sit well with me. It's not that I want them to mess up, but I do want them to understand the possible consequences of not learning effective money management strategies. I want them to have the plan that allowed me to give them a financial head start in their adult lives, ahead of most people their age. I want them to be able to use my system to grow their wealth even more.

I'm teaching my children to handle money with the exact systems and strategies I developed after a lot of trial and error. The strategies I used are completely outlined in this book.

While working with hundreds of clients, it became clear to me that these wealth systems and strategies are more necessary now than ever, as many people are struggling financially. Families all over the world are fighting to keep a roof over their heads and food on the table, with little left over to build real wealth.

The average age of first-time homebuyers is increasing every year. A generation ago, kids in their twenties were able to scrape together down payments to make home purchases. Today, those first-time homebuyers are closer to forty. According to the National Association of Realtors, the share of first-time homebuyers is the lowest it has been since 1981.

I refuse to believe that the American Dream of opportunity and prosperity has died. Actually, I'm proof that it hasn't. With the strategies and systems in this book, I was able to achieve, in my twenties, what most are just starting to work on in their thirties. Financially, I am now in a position in my early forties that most do not reach until their early sixties.

Some of this achievement was due to the fact that I had faced some significant struggles in my late teens and early twenties. My mother died in a catastrophic plane accident. The impact of her death and the subsequent consequences of my actions took me to rock bottom emotionally at an age when most of my peers were excitedly planning for their college years with great anticipation and personal growth opportunities. They were launching into adulthood as I was crashing and burning. I missed seventy-six days of school in my senior year of high school.

It took me five and a half years to get an associate's degree in college. I was more focused on trying to become the top-ranking SOCOM US Navy Seals player in the world, a video game that I played a lot. I managed to rank as high as number three in the world.

Gaming, drugs, and alcohol gave me relief from the emotional struggles I was experiencing. I wasn't a bad person, but I wasn't excelling in life either. Being in a poor emotional state was causing me to make poor financial decisions.

I hit rock bottom financially in my late twenties. I was taking care of my money. I just didn't have enough of it. I found it necessary to focus on my family more than my business. My business expenses stayed the same, but I didn't work as much. Instead, I spent time caring for my family and figuring out who I needed to be as a husband and father.

My "aha moment" occurred when my son was born. I already had a toddler. Looking at my daughter and my newborn son, it hit me that I didn't want to live at rock bottom anymore. I could choose to live a different life. I decided that I would do whatever it took to step up and be a more responsible husband and father. I wanted to provide a financially stable life for all of us.

It was a rude awakening to discover the depth of the financial hole I had dug for myself. But I dropped the shovel I had been digging with and started to climb. I began to analyze everything: my attitude, my values, my skill set, the people in my life, how we handled the little money we had, and how I managed my time. Improvements were needed in all those areas. It was time to improve my business. I started seeking experts, coaches, authors, and advisors who had already achieved more in life than I had so that I could learn from them. I did it by becoming one of the top real estate agents in Indiana.

I don't want to call where I'm at today "the end result" because I'm certainly not finished growing and building, but I am at a point where life is good. My attitude and outlook are more positive than ever. My values are rock solid. The people I have in my life support my vision and add positively to my days. I'm confident in the skills I've gained. I have generated a level of wealth that matches the vision I had when I started climbing out of my deep, dark hole, and I know how to achieve the vision I have today for my family's future. Because of this, I know it is time for this book to come to fruition.

All of my struggles and the lessons I learned led me to realize wealth isn't as much a matter of circumstance as it is a state of mind. Because of that, your definition and mine are likely very different. It's also doubtful that our circumstances from childhood to the present have been the same. Nevertheless, the ultimate goal of this book is to change your awareness of how you currently manage your wealth and adopt a system to do it more effectively so you can achieve your life's vision.

I learned a lot of the strategies in this book the hard way. I don't want that for anyone else. This book delivers the exact blueprint I used on my wealth journey and continue to use today. I hope you don't consider it a quick read. I prefer to think of it as a textbook. I will ask you a lot of questions throughout to stimulate your thinking and awareness around wealth. I've also included very specific exercises and homework for you to do if you choose to follow in my footsteps. Please note that the heavy lifting is in the first part of the book. Don't let it discourage you because once you get your foundation right, the rest becomes easier.

This book is for my kids, loved ones, clients and associates, and you. Life is so much better when you're no longer worried about money, when how much you have or don't have doesn't decide how you're going to deal with situations that arise in your life. Our starting points and our visions may be very different, but we are walking a similar path, the path to wealth. Let's get started!

PART ONE

CHAPTER 1

The Cheviron Pyramid of Wealth™

WHEN MY INTERNAL drive to write this book could no longer be ignored, I made some drastic changes to my day-to-day commitments and habits. I locked myself in my home office for sixty days to do nothing but think and write, analyzing my journey, strategies, systems, and the success of myself and others because of them. I was only able to do this because I have my own financial house in order. I didn't have to worry about paying my monthly bills because I was able to finance the time required through my wealth.

My goal was to demonstrate the building blocks I used to get my financial feet under me and grow my net worth. My hope is that by building with those same blocks, you will join those in the top 5 percent of wealth in the world. As of this writing, that means having a net worth between one and two million dollars. Even if you are beginning from a point of scarcity, this wealth plan can help you get your financial house in order so you can begin your journey toward wealth.

During the first thirty days, I did what is called a brain dump. I wrote out all of my thoughts so they could be organized. I kept asking myself this question: "What do my children need to know to achieve true wealth?" I wasn't only thinking about the sexy stuff, like the assets I would suggest they accumulate. Of course, that's part of it. However, the core of what makes the journey to wealth possible has more to do with vision, mindset, and awareness.

As I organized this content, something became vividly clear. I could distinctly see three different sets of building blocks and how they worked together to build wealth. Even better, I could plainly see how those building blocks worked to hold financial wealth together when the inevitable hits came at me personally and in my business.

In my lifetime, I have seen far more people tumble down the metaphorical mountaintop that is wealth than summit its peak. From witnessing those experiences, I knew this book would need to offer something different than other books on the topic of wealth. While I have learned much from the greats of our time who teach positive money habits, I have learned even more from my personal experiences. I began to wonder if the majority of the world was following a plan that just wasn't working anymore. It's been said that the definition of insanity is doing the same thing over and over while expecting a different result. Not everything I tried worked, so I went back to studying what I considered success from my past.

The John Wooden Effect

Being a huge fan of the great UCLA basketball coach John Wooden, I recalled studying the Pyramid of Success he taught his players. The Pyramid of Success was what made them successful, earning ten national championships in twelve years. What I find most interesting is that there are twenty-five blocks within his Pyramid of Success, and only one is about skill. The rest revolve around personal traits and characteristics. I recognized that same pattern in my wealth plan, with less emphasis on the skills and more on becoming a wealthy person in mindset first.

I found it interesting that one of the first things Coach Wooden taught his new players was how to put on their socks and tie their shoes. This may sound ridiculous until you understand that a sock with even a slight wrinkle can cause a giant blister that impedes a player's ability to focus during games. Shoes that come untied can cause a fall that ends a player's career. In basketball and life, getting the fundamentals right makes all the difference in the level of success you achieve. By identifying and prioritizing those fundamentals in your financial life, you'll be unstoppable.

Definition of Success

John Wooden's definition of success is this: "Success is peace of mind, which is a direct result of self-satisfaction in knowing you made the effort to become the best that you are capable of becoming." I believe achieving success on our wealth journey has many similarities. Achieving wealth certainly brings peace of mind and self-satisfaction. And it requires effort.

The question most people fail to consider is where and how to direct their effort.

So, I designed what I call the "Cheviron Pyramid of Wealth," which contains the building blocks I found necessary to help anyone achieve their vision of wealth. It contains twenty-two blocks divided into three parts.

The first set of blocks creates a solid foundation for the rest. This is where the bulk of the work will be. It's personal. It's where you get a handle on your current financial situation and direct your money where it needs to go to support the vision you have for your future.

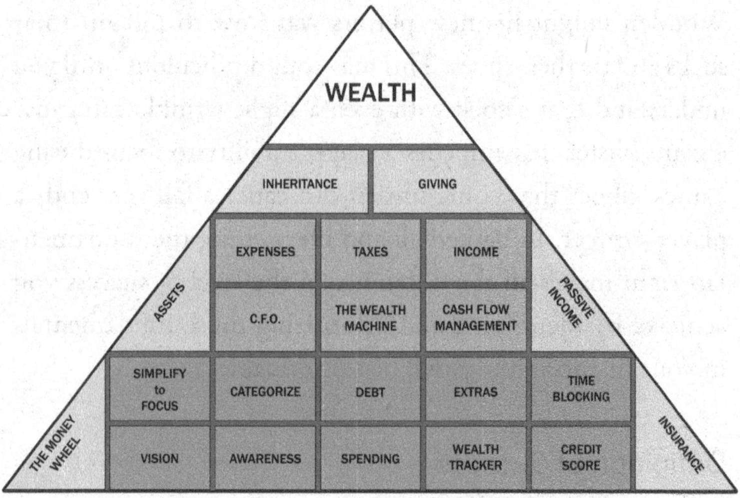

Getting this first part right addressed nearly 50 percent of my previous financial challenges. This is where we will address questions like these:

- How do you define your vision for wealth?
- What do you think about money?

- How do you take care of your money?
- How do you spend your money?
- What is your net worth?
- How do you handle debt?
- How do you keep it simple?

The next part of the Cheviron Pyramid of Wealth addresses how we think and act as business owners. If you are not currently a business owner, entrepreneur, or hobbyist, you may have to look at this section a little differently. However, I highly recommend reading it, as there are many strategies that cross into personal finances. Owning a business is a vehicle that many of my clients and I have relied on to create much of our personal wealth. If nothing else, learning to think like an entrepreneur might inspire you to become one.

The last part of the pyramid includes the pieces on the outside that hold it all together. Having seen too many people lose everything when hard times hit, this part is near and dear to my heart. On the opposite end of that spectrum, I've known many who have created generational wealth by operating successfully with the information provided in the final section of the pyramid. The only difference is this: If your base isn't solidly in place, the chances of it tumbling down increase. And that is why we start with a solid foundation, to ensure we build it to last forever.

As you move forward on your personal journey to wealth, you will start by mastering the basics. They're not very hard to do, but they must be done. Some are even pretty simple, but I wouldn't say they're easy. Some of them may require a bit more commitment than you might expect. I beg you not to skip those basic steps because if you don't get them right, you won't get where you want to go. It would be like a builder ignoring cracks in a foundation and continuing to build anyway. The wealth pyramid has the same building requirements as building a structure. All the blocks must be present to build a strong foundation. Without them, you create a risk for serious damage that will demand repair later. Allowing that to happen is why more people fall down the mountain of wealth than summit it. When you do get the initial steps right, your journey to wealth will be much smoother and more fulfilling.

CHAPTER 2

Vision

WHEN MY DAUGHTER, became a teenager, she developed an addiction to shopping. I have since learned this is a common plague of teenage girls. Dads are usually the last to figure these things out. It seemed that, overnight, my daughter developed a love for Lululemon™ clothing that rivaled a human's need for oxygen. I am convinced it's her vision to own an entire store's worth.

She participates in competitive cheer, so we travel for those competitions. One of the bonuses, according to her, is the opportunity to visit shopping malls in different cities. Her desire, when entering any new mall, is to find out if they have a Lululemon store. That is her first goal. Her second goal is to locate that store.

Now, my daughter is a lot like me—determined. Once she has a strong desire for something, nothing gets in her way. When it comes to achieving goals, I think we could all take notes from my daughter's playbook.

Here's what I have observed with my daughter and her goal of finding Lululemon in every city we visit. She does her research to locate the closest or sometimes the largest mall. This helps her get started on the right path. The challenge with going to a new mall is that we don't usually know which entrance will take us closest to my daughter's ultimate destination. So, the first stop for her is the directory. Finding the location of the store is pretty easy. Once found, the next step is to figure out where to start, that big red star that seems to be on all mall directories. Once my daughter finds our starting point and our destination, she outlines the most direct route. She has a vision of owning something new from Lululemon, she has set a goal to locate the store, and she has determined the best path to get there. These are all basic steps in goal setting. Yay for her.

Now, here's the thing I have found to be very interesting while watching my daughter work toward this simple goal. My daughter is smart, and she understands it's not going to be a straight path. There are going to be hurdles, obstacles, and people in her life who interfere.

My daughter isn't always successful in reaching her goals quickly. When shopping with the family, her biggest obstacle is her brother. He likes to look at sneakers, and we'll inevitably have to stop at a sneaker store on the way to Lululemon. Another potential obstacle is passing a Starbucks. My wife, Lynsee, will want to stop there if it is before 2 p.m.

Rather than letting these obstacles upset her, my daughter keeps her end goal in focus, knowing these delays are just part of the journey. They're not stopping her from achieving what she wants. That's an important lesson I wish all the people I train would learn. That's how we all need to be with our goals: determined, tenacious, and driven, willing to work around obstacles, no matter how big, in anticipation of what's coming.

The achievement of our goals is rarely straightforward. If we knew exactly every step to get from here to there, we'd probably already be there. We set goals for things we don't have yet and should expect to learn new things or even overcome obstacles to achieve them. Encountering obstacles along the path to your goal doesn't mean you give up! They are not stopping points. They are only traffic lights or detours.

Back to my daughter's story: Eventually, we reach Lululemon, and she is ecstatic. She gets to see, touch, and feel her favorite clothing, check out new styles and colors, and often leaves the store with a purchase. She has achieved her goal! I am happy, too, as the cost of the purchase is well worth the value of seeing my daughter become "a natural" at setting and achieving her goal. As someone who relies on the same qualities my daughter demonstrated to achieve her wardrobe goals, I'm hopeful that these qualities will transfer to her financial responsibility when the time comes.

Vision versus Goals

For me, *vision* is the big picture of the lifestyle I want to live and provide for my family. My vision is the 50,000-foot view of my life. This is where I picture where I'm going in life, who I want to become, and why I want to be that person.

Reflecting on our life's vision requires us to slow down to assess what is right and what is wrong. It's a time to consider the kind of people we have become and whether we are being true to ourselves. It's when we think about our larger purpose in life. If we have any regrets, can we take steps to release them? Is there something about ourselves we'd like to change? We only get one go-around in life. How do we make it the best?

Goals are the stepping stones to achieving the vision. This is where you zoom in on your life. It's where you can more clearly see the steps you need to take to achieve that broader life vision.

I invest a lot of time thinking about my vision and outlining the goals required to achieve it. How about you? Have you outlined a vision for your future? When was the last time you gave it serious thought? Is it something you review periodically, or do you keep it in mind all the time? If you have outlined your vision, have you broken it down into steps or goals to achieve along the way to success?

If you don't have answers to those questions, I'm here to help. After all, how can you achieve something if you don't know exactly what it is you'd like to achieve and how to get from where you are to where you want to be?

The first person who taught me about writing goals was Brian Buffini, my first real estate mentor. He helped me understand how to create a foundation for business and life. He taught that we should write goals in five areas of our life: Spiritual, Personal, Family, Business, and Financial. He did not teach any particular order or give any one area more weight. The order of importance is something we all need to determine for ourselves.

Personally, I give the most weight to my spiritual goals. If I don't get my spiritual life right, it doesn't matter what's happening with the other categories. After years of observation, it's my opinion that this is where a lot of people get things wrong. They focus, first and foremost, on their financial goals, weighing everything else as less important. The result of this is often less attention to emotional health, physical health, and family relationships. What's the point of getting the money right if everything else falls apart?

I remember the first time I wrote my goals. I had no clue what I was doing, why I was doing it, if I was even doing it right, or what my vision was. I only knew what my vision of my future wasn't. It wasn't the life I was living at that time. I struggled to picture that 50,000-foot view. Heck, I could barely envision the next two steps. And maybe that's where you start, too. Maybe you picked up this book because you're just not happy with your current financial situation and are looking for some answers to get somewhere else.

One of the biggest challenges I encounter when coaching people is their preconceived notions about goal setting. Perhaps they've given it a try once or twice and then given up. I often hear things like, "I've done that," or "I've heard that before." Let me caution you about thinking this is a chapter to skip. If you're serious about achieving your definition of wealth, whatever that is, I'm going to ask you to go deep into your whole life's vision. I'm going to ask you to do the work necessary to set realistic, achievable goals for which you will develop a structured plan to get from here to there.

Getting good at developing your life plan and setting goals to achieve it is the foundation of everything you need to get from here to wealth. This is the keystone. It's the central part of the system covered in the rest of this book. Everything you learn here depends on getting this first part right.

Goal setting is one of the base blocks of our foundation for wealth. And, if you've ever watched anything being built, a home or commercial building, the beginning phase isn't sexy. There's a lot of digging and dirt, and it all just looks messy. And that's okay. The important thing is that they have a blueprint to follow. It contains both the vision and its breakdown into goals. When the foundational work is done right, the end result will stand the test of time.

Understanding Goals

When I talk with clients in my coaching business, we start with them telling me what they're struggling with. These struggles may range from a belief that they aren't making enough money to issues with aligning their work with the lifestyle they desire. When I ask what they want most, the typical response is, "To know how to get to the next level."

As a coach, my job involves actively listening and asking insightful questions to help my clients explore their thoughts, feelings, and options to gain a deeper understanding of their needs. After listening to their struggles, I typically ask questions like these:

- What does that next level look like?
- What is your vision beyond that level?

- Why is this vision important to you?
- What resources or skills do you have today to help you achieve your vision?

Identifying the gap between where they are today and where they want to go is the key to clarifying the steps they need to take. Identifying their motivation is what will keep them moving forward when striving for that next level gets hard. Unfortunately for them, we can't use *my* drive and motivation to get them where they want to go. It has to be *their* motivation.

The birth of my first child, my daughter, made me recognize the need to change my financial path, but it was the birth of my son that motivated me to finally act and do what needed to be done. Now, I don't necessarily recommend having a child to create motivation in life. Having a child, someone who was wholly dependent on my support, gave me my "why." Achieving my new vision became essential to taking the best care possible of my wife and children. That motivation served as a starting point for achieving many future goals. However, at that point in my life, I didn't really understand goal setting. To get from where I was to where I wanted to be required clear, written goals. I learned that there are several reasons we use goals as a tool for building wealth.

- Goals motivate us. When we lack motivation, it gets a little tougher to do the work we need to do. When we start each day by reviewing our goals, it gets us on track. It helps us to keep what's important front and center from the moment we wake up and carries us throughout our days.
- Goals compound. Every goal achieved makes us better people. We get better at refining our vision. We grow

and become more confident in our abilities to climb to greater heights.

- Goals help us create a map to what we want, which shows us our priorities. They help us focus, like my daughter finding her way to Lululemon.

When we don't have clear, written goals, these things happen:

- In the absence of clear goals, there is no sense of accomplishment. When we have written goals, even small victories create momentum.
- Written goals support our motivations. Without motivation, we risk becoming stagnant. Without movement, it can be too easy to settle or even wallow where we began.
- Without clear goals, we risk becoming a passenger, instead of the driver, on our journey. If we rely on someone else, it's unlikely they're going where we want to go. With goals, we take control of our destination.

Here's an example of a goal written as I thought goals were supposed to be written versus the better way I know today.

Early form of writing goals:

- Spiritual: Attend church every week
- Family: Home by 5 p.m. and attend 80 percent of kids' events/sports
- Business: Income $137,500, sales $5,132,512, units 42, NO OPEN HOUSES!
- Financial: Net worth, $120,000
- Personal: Weight 165, exercise 3 times a week

How I write those goals today with greater detail:

- Spiritual: Read a passage from the Bible as part of my morning routine and reflect on its meaning in my life. Engage mentally and emotionally in church services every week.
- Family: Be home by 5 p.m. daily to enjoy dinner with the family. Attend a minimum of 80 percent of the kids' events/sports.
- Business: Serve my clients well and generate a total income of $137,500 by selling $5,133,000 in real estate without scheduling appointments on Sundays.
- Financial: Increase my worth to $120,000 by adding $60,000 of assets to my portfolio and reducing my debt by $60,000.
- Personal: Achieve my weight goal of 165 pounds by eliminating fast food and reducing portion sizes, as well as working out for ninety minutes at the gym three times per week.

The individual details I added to my goals helped me to compartmentalize, into small victories, what I needed to do to achieve the overall goal. Small victories were attainable, less overwhelming, and, ultimately, motivating. I could actually see and feel what achieving them would be like. My goals became a storyline in my head all day, every day.

Organization and Focus

When it comes to achieving goals, two of my superpowers are organization and focus. I excel at taking large subjects and boiling them down to what is most important or breaking them down into steps that are small enough to manage. Relying on that ability, I eventually broke down the process of achieving wealth into the building blocks I used for my personal journey. For this, I created the pyramid illustration introduced in Chapter 1. I organized these steps into a specific order, a plan. After using this plan for myself and with my coaching clients, I formalized it into what I call the Cheviron Pyramid of Wealth. It's the system you will be learning and using throughout this book. I'll explain it in more detail in Chapter 3, but let's review that building block of vision and goals first.

To develop your organization and focus on achieving your wealth goals, I'm going to lay out some exercises that you will need to do. This is the "work" I referred to earlier. It is a necessary part of getting from here to wherever you want to be with regard to your wealth.

It's essential to answer all the questions in this chapter to begin building your wealth plan. If you fail to answer those questions about your vision, goals, and what motivates you, the rest of this book will not serve you well. You must fully identify *your* goals, *your* desires, and *your* dreams. Having a strong desire and an uncomplicated picture of what you want will become your North Star, your guiding light to help you pull through when the work feels too hard.

One of the most important elements of achieving goals is to write them down. In fact, in this chapter, you shouldn't just read the material. I strongly advise you to use a journal, notebook, or some other device to do the work I'll outline here. Why do I advise you to write them down? When you write them down and read them back, you will develop an even clearer picture of what you really want.

Motivational speaker and self-development author Brian Tracy tells the story of advising a young man at one of his seminars to write down one hundred and one goals. The young man did as he was told and set the list aside. Twelve years later, he was going through some papers and came across his list. He was amazed to see that he had achieved all of them. According to Mr. Tracy, when we write our goals, they become programmed into our subconscious, which works on them twenty-four hours a day. Now, I believe in reviewing my goals daily, and find they are achieved much faster than the time frame in that story. There is something about getting your thoughts and ideas out of your head and having them where you can read them that brings you several steps closer to having them become reality. They are more prominent in your thoughts, which allows you to notice opportunities that contribute to their achievement.

It is best if you commit to doing this work in a quiet place, by yourself, without distractions. Distractions will kill your concentration and prevent you from working toward your goals. My advice to all of my clients is to invest time in ninety-minute increments to think about their goals. When I do this, I actually set a countdown clock. That way, I subconsciously know I am working against the clock and need to complete the task at hand in a timely manner.

After ninety minutes, it's time to step away from those goals. Take a break for a day or two but come back to them at a later date. It's amazing how, after you've had a break from thinking about your goals, you can dig deeper into what you want your future to look like and why. This is when to consider if those goals are *really* what you want or if they can be improved upon. You'll also consider whether what you've written is truly *your* goal, not something you think you should want or something that might please others when you accomplish it. Do you really want to take a Hawaiian vacation, or are you setting that goal because your spouse or family wants it?

Work on them some more, then take another break. The third and last time you work on your vision and goals will be to gain complete clarity and simplification so you can laser-focus your attention on them. You may find yourself removing things you initially thought you wanted. It happens. It's called evolution. As we refine our thinking, our desires change.

EXERCISE:

Below is the first set of questions I want you to answer in writing. You can write your answers in bullet points as brief thoughts. Some people find it works better for them to write out a descriptive paragraph. Whatever method you choose, you will end up with the same results. Now, set a timer for ten minutes to write down everything that comes to mind as an answer to this first question. There's no judgment here. You don't need to share your answers with anyone. Just write down what you feel in your head and heart are solid answers to the question:

What does wealth mean to you?

____

____

____

____

____

____

Having asked dozens of people, "What does wealth mean to you?" I learned that there are as many answers as there are people. It's not the same thing for you as it is for me or even for your closest loved ones. The definition of wealth doesn't depend on a number but rather on a feeling. Sure, when we think of wealth, we might picture experiences or things that require money. However, the feelings those experiences and things produce are the real wealth.

For me, that feeling revolves around my family. Does my wealth provide well for my family? Does it allow me to invest quality time with them? Am I happy when I'm with them? Am I happy overall? How is my health? Can I physically participate in family activities? Please know, if your health is not good, it's really hard to consider yourself wealthy or to become wealthy. Am I having fun? No matter what I'm doing, am I enjoying it? And last, am I living with purpose?

The next feeling of wealth for me is about freedom. Am I free of time, or is my time committed or obligated to someone or something else? Am I free of the need to continue exchanging my time for money? Am I free from having to live in a specific location? By this, I mean having the option to live anywhere or nowhere, moving about the planet as I wish. The choices are endless.

Another key aspect of wealth, for me, is my legacy. How do I ensure that, when my time on earth is over, the energy that I've spent creating wealth serves a good purpose? How does it continue?

I could have filled this entire book with examples of what wealth means to me, to my loved ones, my business associates, friends, and so on. But the best use of your time wouldn't be to read them. Instead, my goal is that you discover what wealth means to you.

The next question for you to answer in writing is this*: At the end of your working career, whenever that is, where must you be financially?* This time, set your timer for fifteen minutes. For most of the people I work with, this one takes a bit more time to think through.

____

____

____

____

____

____

Begin by deciding when you want to end your working career. When I say "working career," I don't mean work as a whole, but specifically, when will you be done with the commitment of exchanging time for money? Is it once you've achieved something in particular in your career? Is it a specific date or age? Is it when you've accumulated a certain amount of money or set up enough passive income to support your lifestyle? Some of the questions I'll ask have multiple layers, and I'm asking you to invest the time necessary to discover what they mean to you.

My questions for you are just the starting point. If and when other questions arise around the thoughts they generate, follow that trail of questions until you've exhausted all the ones you can think of. Continue to write your answers to capture all those key thoughts.

I don't know where you are in life at this moment: your physical location, your age, your health, or your career. I can tell you, though, that most of my clients are in America. My favorite clients are in their mid-fifties. That's because in our country, most people retire in their sixties. So, when they get into the fifty to fifty-five age range, they get serious about figuring out their retirement years. They start to "feel the pressure of the clock ticking." The drive that comes from the fear of not living the life of their dreams gets stronger. They go all in on whatever needs to be done. When this happens, the results take half the time they would otherwise. The satisfaction of building momentum is a win for both of us. If you're younger than that, I am excited to know that the light bulb in your mind has turned on to determine what wealth means to you and that you are open to doing the work to achieve it.

Note that if you are in your twenties, you may find it challenging to answer some of these questions, and that's okay. It's likely you haven't given it much thought at this point in your life. It's possible that you don't have enough work or life experience or have faced enough challenges to see the possibilities yet. It doesn't mean you can't try to do the work. Consider what your elders have done or are doing and what you do or don't want in your life based on their experiences. Understand that your initial thoughts on these questions will likely change over the next five or ten years, and that's okay, too. Just start outlining a rough picture now. It will come into focus eventually.

You may be more concerned with how you will survive today or how you can make it through this year. That's fine. Remember that all the smaller things you do help to build the bigger picture you are trying to achieve. You can apply the same strategies for success to anything you want.

The vision guiding me for the last twelve years is to be free when my son graduates from high school. My freedom, which is part of my wealth, revolves around three things covered in this chapter:

1. Freedom of location, which means I can work anywhere without location constraints.
2. Freedom of time, which means I am not bound by limitations on my schedule.
3. Free of money. At first, my goal was to simply have enough financial stability to live the life I desired without needing to earn money to sustain it. But as I deepened

> my understanding of wealth, that goal evolved. I no longer wanted to be consumed by thoughts of what to charge for my services. I realized I had become a prisoner not to money itself, but to the desire and constant calculation around earning it.

The next question for you to consider is this: *What can you achieve in the next twelve months to take a step in the right direction?* Give yourself ten minutes of distraction-free time to write out your answer.

____

____

____

____

____

____

You are reading this book to be transformed into someone that you are not today. You are looking for ways to become a wealthy person. My job is to help you determine what that means to you and carve out the right path. Suppose your definition of wealth is dramatically different from where you are today. In that case, this question will help you break that goal down into more precise actions that you can actually begin implementing today.

The next question is this: *What financial improvement would make the most significant difference in your life if you could achieve it within thirty days of reading this book and completing the exercises?*

____

____

____

____

____

____

Would it simply be a matter of having your finances organized? Would it be trimming down your expenses? Is there a specific amount of money you feel would make the difference you seek? What would make you feel that you're getting a handle on your finances or making forward progress? Be specific.

What you are likely to find when answering these four questions is that you have a new awareness. New ideas will hit you, things you've never given thought to in the past. You may think of obstacles in your way or wonder how you can possibly achieve *that* when you're beginning from *here.* Addressing those things is part of the work we will do in the rest of this book.

There may be gaps between what you first think you want and what you decide you really want. And that's okay. You are creating forward momentum. The path you see right now may shift, or even split, as you move forward, but you *are* moving forward, and that's a win that will create the motivation you need for the next steps.

CHAPTER 3

Awareness

NOW THAT YOU have a vision, let's figure out why you're not there yet. This is where we will examine how you think about money and why. I'm going to ask you to go back in time and identify what experiences in your life impacted how you think about and handle your money, as well as your day-to-day thinking about wealth.

What is your relationship with money? Any and all of your past experiences with money contribute to how you think about and handle money today. What has happened in your life that contributed to your current relationship with it? Give this some serious thought. What are your first memories of money? How did you handle money as a kid? How did you see others around you handle it?

I have found it interesting that of all the topics I cover on wealth, this one stands out the most for those who take my online training and those I coach in person. Some of the stories people have told me about their childhood experiences around money amaze me. And the impact of those stories amazes them as we go through this topic of awareness. People are walking around all over the world, handling their money this way or that, and never considering why they do it or if there might be a better way.

A good friend of mine opened my eyes to this subject. She said, "It's not who *taught you* about money, necessarily, Austin. It's *who you learned from about money.*" I had one of those lightbulb moments when this sank in. We are always either *proactively learning*, like when we take a class about finance or wealth, or *reactively learning* when we observe others.

Even if you're not necessarily trying to be aware of what others are doing, you do subconsciously pick up on what's happening around you on every topic of interest. For most of us, our observations come first from the people around us, whom we trust, like family members.

A lot of people around my age were influenced by the Depression-era generation with the mentality that money and other resources are scarce. Many of that generation experienced fear of risk and lived with an intense feeling that they had to protect their resources. The Great Depression left emotional scars on people who then taught their children and grandchildren their ways. While a certain level of risk aversion has value, understanding that attitude about money and wealth is not necessarily relevant to these times and your life today. Those lessons served another generation well, so it's critical that you weigh them against your reality and today's times.

Grandma Clem

The first person who taught me about money was my Grandma Clem. With the exception of two weekends per year, she hosted a family dinner at her house every Saturday night. She fed twenty or more people for over twenty years. There was always room at the table for more, such as neighbors or friends. To her, this gathering was a time to get family right. She was a great role model in that respect.

As an adult, I realize how much time, effort, and cost are involved in feeding so many people each week. How did she do it? She didn't have a lot of money or many sources of it. She used coupons, counted her pennies, and shopped carefully. Sometimes, I'd go to the grocery store with her and watch how she analyzed her choices to get the most out of every penny.

Grandma Clem once told me I was the only grandchild who was like her. I thought it was because she and I both have dominant personalities. Later, I realized it was because we both analyzed everything before a penny or dime was ever spent. All purchases had to be utilitarian.

She would often take me to the bank with her. Having always been a saver, I got a thrill from seeing my bank balance grow, even if it meant I was a very young penny pincher. I used a check ledger to keep track of my money. I received a dopamine hit every time I saw the numbers in that ledger increase. Today, I get the same feeling when I log into my banking app.

By the age of ten, I had saved $1,000. How many ten-year-olds do you know who have that even today? I was always looking for ways to make money: cutting people's lawns, doing other yard work, or whatever neighbors needed done, because I had such a strong desire to see those numbers increase. Growing my bank account brought me feelings of accomplishment, self-confidence, and independence. "Having enough" wasn't something I relied on someone else to do.

Grandma also taught me that money had many meanings. It was to be cared for. She would give me money as gifts and coins to collect. She was a great steward of money. She taught me that there were emotions around money. When we went to the bank, she would get fifty-cent pieces and Susan B. Anthony dollar coins to give to people, including me. These coins were to be enjoyed for what they were, and not necessarily for their dollar value. They weren't to be spent or deposited in a savings account but savored.

What are your stories and feelings about money? Everyone has some feelings about growing their savings, investments, and retirement accounts. As I came to recognize that there were feelings attached to money, I also realized not everyone felt the same as I did. Sadly, as I teach this program around the country, I'm learning that a lot of people have bad feelings and relationships around money. If you have strong negative emotions around getting ahead financially, what do you think the chances are that you will do it? This is so important to understand and think about.

The Scarcity Mindset

I would say that 90 percent of the people I've taught have told me that when it comes to money, they have feelings of fear or scarcity. They worry about not having enough, or they have lived for some portion of their life without enough. When those are the sentiments toward money, it's highly likely you'll make bad decisions with it. For example, you might be so fearful of taking risks that you never really put your money to work for you. You might hoard it in a savings account that earns little interest instead of considering other options. Or you may take too long to act on financial opportunities that come your way and miss out.

While fear may prevent you from making risky financial decisions, that aversion will also prevent you from investing, making your money work for you, and creating true wealth. Of the remaining 10 percent of people I talk with, 5 percent who have significant wealth, are not facing the reality that they don't handle the money well. That leaves just 5 percent with a positive mental outlook when it comes to money. They actively seek opportunities to put their money to work for them beyond holding it in a savings account. When you gain the confidence that comes from managing your money well, you'll make more lucrative decisions along your journey to wealth.

Delayed Gratification

Once I realized what a positive relationship I had with money, I learned to invest it. My goal was always to find ways to make more money with my money. When I was sixteen, I had a truck. My truck was a utility, a tool, for achieving my financial goals.

I remember my second accident with that truck. (We won't talk about the first one.) The back end was badly dented, but it still ran great. Rather than fixing the truck when I got the insurance check for the damages, I saved that money for something bigger, taking advantage of delayed gratification. In my third accident, the truck was hit on the rear quarter panel. Again, it looked terrible but still ran well. If that truck had feelings, I'm sure it wouldn't have been too proud of its appearance. Again, because I only looked at it as a utilitarian vehicle, I didn't pay for repairs with the insurance money. I invested it by opening a credit builder account at my bank.

Unlike most teens I knew, I rarely "spent" money. I bought my first house at age eighteen. In fact, I had to be excused from school to sign the closing papers. When I was asked what I did for work, I had to tell them I was still in high school and didn't have a full-time job. My dad co-signed the loan, but I wrote the check for the down payment because I had it in savings. I didn't know anything about owning real estate; it was just that everyone talked about what a good investment it was. And it turned out to be a good one. I lived there for five years and sold it for a profit.

I was always looking for ways to invest my money to make it work for me. Think about yourself at that age. How would you have handled that money and why? More than likely, how you handled it was due to two things: first, how you were taught to handle money, and second, how you are naturally wired.

Being Guarded with Your Money

One of the habits I find, for a lot of people, is that they treat their wealth like they treat their ex. What do I mean? When we talk about wealth and money, their mindset about it creates a negative feeling in them. Maybe there have been bad past experiences that make them overly cautious. Perhaps there's a lack of trust in how things will turn out when considering investment opportunities. Fortunately, I don't have an ex, and never want to, but I have experienced a lot of negativities around money, too.

My mom died in a small plane crash when I was seventeen. As my parents were divorced at that time, a close family friend was listed as the beneficiary of Mom's life insurance policy. She promised that when the money came in, she would sign the check over to help cover Mom's funeral expenses. Believe it or not, it was my Grandma Clem who paid to bury my mother. Grandma Clem was my father's mother, not my mother's.

Over a year later, we learned that the check had been sent to Mom's friend and cashed. When we contacted this friend about it, her response was, "What check?" Now, please understand that we had been in communication with this woman over the course of the year since my mother's passing. She was like a second mother to me. It was crystal clear what needed to be done with the check when it came in.

Emotionally, that experience gutted me. It took decades to recover from the pain, the loss of trust, and the feeling that money can be the ruin of relationships, especially at times of death. That experience taught me many more lessons than any positive experiences I've had. One such lesson is that I need to protect any money I receive. Another is that I need to proactively direct any inheritance. More on that in Chapter 22.

Family Influence

These essential teachings from Grandma Clem, my father, and my negative experience with my mother's beneficiary bring up the importance of familial influence in your overall attitude about money. Did you live in an environment where your family was super frugal? Or was yours the family that spent money freely? Or was life more like a roller coaster? When money came in, life was good and a lot of spending happened, but once it was gone, times were tough. Was money managed well, or was some spending done for show? I've had neighbors who appeared to be doing quite well with their new cars, boats, and lavish vacations, only to learn that they were up to their eyeballs in debt. It was all superficial.

Did your family have money available for fun experiences or things, or was money always tight? What did you think about money and wealth growing up? What were the actions around money that you saw in others who influenced you?

Were you told that "wealth is the root of all evil"? I have encountered some clients with plenty of money, yet they carry around a sense of guilt about it. They feel guilty that they've done well while loved ones have not. These people often feel their best about their money when they're giving it away to charities or helping a family member. Even when helping others, they might still carry some guilt.

One woman told me that she was raised in a religion where she was taught that money was evil. When she became aware of how this message was influencing her money habits, she thanked me. She didn't want her daughter to grow up with the same feelings and was taking action to change.

How about this one: "Rich people are greedy." If you currently carry that belief, you're probably not super motivated to achieve wealth. No one wants to be perceived as greedy.

What did your family and others who were close to you teach you? Whatever those experiences, know they impact how you think and handle your money today. No matter what your past experience, my goal is for you to develop a positive feeling about money, to understand how to control it, and make it work for you. I want to help you overcome the impact your previous experiences with money have had on how you relate to it today. The sooner you realize that life always happens *for us* and not *to us*, the sooner you can recover and use the lessons to move forward.

What is Inside You?

Reflecting on my life experiences, I am aware of who I am and what's inside me. I understand why I think the way I do and the reasons I take certain actions around wealth. I believe the ability to achieve wealth, no matter your definition, is within everyone. I used the book *The Millionaire Next Door* by Thomas J. Stanley as a simple guide to wealth. It covers the fact that most of the truly wealthy in America are not celebrities or CEOs but average people who handle their money well. Awareness is the first step to opening your mind to the possibilities, liabilities, and opportunities around you.

There's a story I refer to all the time. It's called "Acres of Diamonds" by Russell Conwell. In this story, an African farmer wanted greater wealth. He decided to sell his land, take the money, and travel the world to find his fortune. Not finding it, he returned home only to learn that one of the richest diamond mines ever discovered was on the property he had owned. The farmer had what he wanted all along but went looking for his wealth elsewhere. Isn't that the truth in life for so many people? They're always looking elsewhere, following those "shiny objects" to find what they believe is missing. In my opinion, if more people invested the time to increase their awareness of who they are and what opportunities are available to them, they'd find that the achievement of their goals is easier than expected.

Do the work here and now. Think back through your childhood and early adult years. What did you do well? Where did you fail? Or maybe you didn't fail but learned you could have achieved an even better result if you handled something differently. What tendencies are you still carrying today because of past experiences? What skills have you developed from the past that are serving you well today? What other skills might you need to develop to take you to the next level?

Your Current Money Habits

When it comes to your money habits and how they were formed, I like to think of them like the layers of an onion. It's time to peel them back and get to the root of your habits. Go deep within your memory bank to recall those experiences in detail. Analyze the whys of what happened, the emotions attached to the situations, and how they might continue to influence you today.

As with anything, if you keep doing the same things over and over, you're going to keep getting the same results. Change is in your future if you are serious about furthering your wealth journey. Now, I understand that change can be fearful for some people. Hopefully, that's not you. I'm hoping that the goals you set for achieving wealth will motivate you to look forward to making changes to your habits.

To get started thinking about this, let's review some options:

1. Do you track your finances, or do you ignore them? What I find with a lot of my clients is that the worse their financials are, the less likely they are to track them. They just don't want to acknowledge they're in bad shape. I want you to become so uncomfortable with your finances today that you'll look forward to changing.
2. Is your financial information stored in one place, or is it scattered? This includes your tax records, expenses, and income information. Could someone else open a single document or drawer and find everything quickly and easily?
3. Do you focus more on increasing your income or lowering your expenses? Which has more of your attention? If I gave you an hour to work on one or the other, which would you choose?
4. Do you invest first, or do you invest what's left over? Changing my habit to invest first is what's made the most significant difference in my life. By practicing the habit of investing what's left over, how much will that

be for most people? Zero. It's just too easy to spend everything we have.

5. Do you purchase now, or do you delay gratification? We all get that high, that dopamine hit, from making purchases, from having something new in our lives. The habit I've developed around purchases is to put the item in my online shopping cart, but rarely do I purchase it. I'm sure online retailers are not fans of this habit, but I find that if I wait out making a purchasing decision, more often than not, I realize I don't really want it. But I got that high from the shopping experience. I feel like I bought it because I can see it in my cart, but my money is still in my bank account. Win-win!
6. Do you buy things, or do you buy experiences? Neither answer is right or wrong. With this one, figure out which is your habit. It's important to note that it's also important to determine which habit your significant other prefers. If you don't have the same habit, you could have some issues when you decide to make some changes to your buying habits.
7. Are you a purchaser or an investor? If I were to give you a substantial amount of cash today to do with what you wish, would you buy things, or would you invest the money in your future or a goal? An experience I had with this was with my Grandpa Ralph. Before he passed away, he gave all his kids the bulk of their inheritance to be able to watch what they would do with it. My sister and I split my mother's share. When my grand-

father asked me what I would do with it, my answer was "invest it." When I showed the check to my wife, she asked, "What are we going to buy with it?" My answer was "stocks" or "real estate." All I could think was, "How can I use this to help me achieve the vision I truly desire?"

8. Do you treat money as if it's scarce or abundant? Do you worry you won't have enough, or are you more likely to give to others from your abundance? I remember working for my dad and writing checks for him. He was always receiving requests for money donations. He would always give something. I remember thinking that we didn't have a lot of money ourselves and wondering why he'd give it away.

What I discovered was that he had an abundance mindset, and at that time, my mindset was one where money was scarce. I was thinking about how we could keep what we had and protect it. His thinking was, "I can always make more. Maybe these people need it more than I do right now." When you can change your mindset to one of abundance, I promise that your world will completely change.

The bottom line is that money is nothing more than a tool. It's something you earn and care for, so it works for you the way you want it to.

EXERCISE:

Identify one or more of your past experiences around money and consider how it shows up in your life today. Once you are aware of it, determine whether it's serving you as you strive to achieve greater wealth.

PART TWO

CHAPTER 4

Spending

IN THIS BLOCK of the Cheviron Pyramid of Wealth, we are going to roll up our sleeves and find out exactly where your money goes. You might think you know this already, but do you? I will warn you now that this is going to be the toughest chapter in the book. Yet, the work you'll do here will make the most significant difference in your wealth journey. If you do not get your spending in line, it won't matter how much money you make. You can't get control over what goes out until you know where it's going. It's imperative that you know where you let your money go.

Note the phrase "where you let your money go." Your money does not have a conscious mind, and it cannot choose to run off. It cannot decide whether to buy an eighty-inch television or a luxury vehicle. Those decisions are yours. It's time to see where you might make better choices.

Think of your money as a three-year-old. You wouldn't let them run off just anywhere, would you? You protect and guide them. You consider their future. You make conscious decisions about how you will shape them into productive adults. As you have a job to care for your children, it's your job to be the guardian of your money, to protect it and plan for its future.

The Lack of Good Stewardship

It's funny that most people, when asked, "What would you do with $10,000 if I handed it to you right now?" have quick answers. They have places for it to go. Some will pay bills. Others would take a grand vacation. Rarely do we hear people say, "I'd put it in savings," or "I'd invest it." That $10,000 would be spent almost as quickly as it was handed over. That's because they don't have a vision or a plan.

What usually happens when there's an increase in income is that our spending increases proportionally. It's the financial version of Parkinson's Law. That law states that work expands to fill the available time. When it comes to extra or newfound money, our spending tends to expand to use all available.

When we don't feel that we have enough, we tell ourselves, "When I make more, I'll do—" whatever you think is missing. We are mentally spending money we don't have. When we finally get that increase in income, we loosen up our spending to an amount equal to the increase. When that happens, it's as if the money evaporates, and we remain in the same frame of mind: "I don't have enough." To work toward wealth, the mindset must be more like, "I'm going to work on managing my money better, no matter how much I have."

We've all heard the stories of people who became multi-millionaires despite never earning a high income. Some have left tremendous amounts of money to charities, the towns they lived in, or helped underprivileged youth attend college. How did that happen? Well, it was possible because they were good stewards of the money they did have.

Not to knock the school system, but I sure would love it if there were mandatory classes on how money works and how to make the most of it. I don't recall a single class that covered anything about being a responsible adult when it comes to handling money. I know my kids don't have those classes today. My kids are the number one reason I worked so hard to build the Cheviron Pyramid of Wealth. My desire for them is to avoid the struggles I faced and learn that money is best saved and invested instead of spent.

The Hard Stuff

Anything worthwhile requires effort. What I'm asking you to do now may involve a commitment of several hours of your time. If you have a significant other, the results of this might force you to have some serious conversations, to choose to make some sacrifices, or to negotiate some middle ground. This is the make-or-break step on the path to wealth.

While it would be nice if people were taught this kind of thing early in life, there's no time like the present to learn. I'm asking you to put pencil to paper or fingers to keyboard and open a spreadsheet. We are going to determine exactly where your money has been going.

When I get into this topic with my clients during live events, I have heard groans and watched as body language changed from expectancy to reluctance. You would think I had just told everyone they were going to have a root canal without anesthesia or that we were going to fill out tax forms as an exercise. In actuality, it's neither. There will be no physical pain. And tax forms are for the benefit of the government. The spreadsheet you'll be creating is 100 percent for your benefit.

If you have neglected reviewing your spending for quite some time, this will be really hard, but also extremely enlightening. Motivational speaker Les Brown says, "Do what is easy, and your life will be hard. Do what is hard, and your life will become easy." With this exercise, you will start to make your life easier around the subject of wealth. That may require you to do what is hard today.

This is where a lot of readers will put this book down. They may fear doing the work. Just the thought of gathering all that information might be overwhelming. Or they may fear what they'll find if they do the work. Avoiding the work now will make life harder later, and I'm guessing that is exactly why you're reading this book now. Like taxes, the longer you wait to complete the forms, the greater the penalty, the greater the angst, and the more difficult it will be to find all the information you need.

If you knew, for a fact, that doing one single exercise would allow you to lessen the time to achieve the vision you created in Chapter 2, wouldn't you want to get started right away? If you're genuinely passionate about your vision, your answer will be "yes." Let's get to it!

The Work

We're going to do the exercise for this chapter now instead of at the end. It's that important. Then, we'll go over what to do with the information you gather.

Step 1: Pull out your statements for every personal account for the last ninety days. This includes your checking account, savings, and credit cards. Also, include any receipts you have where you used cash. You want all the records of where your money went for the last ninety days.

Step 2: List every spend as an individual item. What you want here is the name of the place where the money was spent. Then, in a separate column, list the amount paid. You can do this on a pad of paper or a spreadsheet. In my experience, the spreadsheet is better. It will help you analyze the different categories of spending later.

Even my clients who believe they track their spending well discover something that surprises them during this process. My clients who have neglected tracking their spending are often shocked at how much money has gone into what I call "The Black Hole." There's no retained value for the amount that was used.

Be sure to note if you have any returns. That's money coming back to you. That's always a good thing. You want to credit returns against the bottom line of your spending. Noting this could also give you a clue as to where you are making decisions that are not serving your life. If you see a trend that you are frequently spending money and returning the same type of items to the same store, there is a good chance you really don't need those things. It may be time to rethink whether you really need that product or if you should no longer shop at that particular store.

If you and other family members share a credit card account, you may not know what some of the charges are. You may have to involve them in this research. I'll caution you to stay focused on the documentation of where the money is going. During this exercise, it is not the time to have conversations about why this money was spent. I do understand this could be opening a Pandora's box. And once it is opened, you might need to deal with it. I want you to be very conscious that when you start addressing things you have been hiding, the demons in the closet could begin to come out. Do your best to continue through the work and come back to address your spending list later. For now, we need the list to be completed and tallied.

You will, more than likely, see that your spending fluctuates from month to month. That's normal. In fact, it would be a rare thing to have any two months of spending add up to exactly the same amount.

Step 3: Determine your monthly average of personal expenses by dividing your ninety-day total by three.

If you're like most people, you spend more during a month when you take a vacation. Maybe you spend more in December for the holidays. Or there may have been some oddball expenses, such as needing a significant home repair or car maintenance. That's perfectly normal. In my case, for example, my dog needed two major surgeries over eighteen months. That stuff just happens. You can't plan for it.

The goal for this step is to determine a monthly average spread over three months. That will be your baseline. Once we have that figure, we can start to predict what your next three months of spending might be.

The most important thing about this number is that we will use it as we build your wealth machine. It's part of figuring out how much your salary and/or your business needs to generate to provide for your lifestyle every month. Knowing this number is critical to fulfilling your wealth plan.

I warned you this was going to be a lot of work at first. I know I'm asking a lot, and I have high expectations that you'll do the job. That's because I also know that you are 100 percent committed to your vision and will do whatever it takes to achieve it. I congratulate you for making it this far and promise the work will get easier.

Your Wealth Identity

Once you know where your money goes, realize that your spending habits are part of your identity. You may be the guy or gal wearing the latest trendy clothing or hairstyle. You may be like my daughter with a Lululemon fixation. You might be the friend at happy hour on Friday who buys the first round of drinks. You may be the one offering to drive on weekend getaways in your new car. You may be the fun aunt, uncle, or grandparent who takes the kiddos shopping, to the arcade, the movies, or even Disneyland. Aren't you the best? You have it all. You do it all.

My question to you is this: Can you really afford it all? Have you chosen to spend it all in the present, or are you paying at least some of it forward to your future self? When you don't choose your future, you're going to spend everything you have today and will possibly take on debt that you *will* need to deal with in the future. That's not in your best interest. What I'm saying is that the true cost of today's spending is your future.

Every lifestyle comes with a cost. When your lifestyle negatively impacts your net worth or your future self-sufficiency, it's time to consider a change. What lifestyle really makes sense for you at your current stage of life with your current income? I challenge you to give this serious consideration. Then, study the spreadsheet you've created. Where have you been spending money without really giving it much consideration? Are you making purchases deliberately or out of habit? Again, there is no need to over-analyze. We are just increasing your awareness around your spending habits.

It has become way too easy to tap your debit or credit card or click a button to pay with your phone. How often do you actually look at the total while doing it and pause to think if each purchase serves a true need? Amazon is an excellent example of this. I can make a purchase in less than sixty seconds and have it delivered within forty-eight hours. It's so easy until I look at my credit card statement. How often do you do more than glance at the cost of an item before tossing it in your shopping cart? Do you really use or benefit from all those subscription services you have? You may decide some of your spending is nothing but waste, or maybe even due to a bit of laziness. Sure, it's easier to pick up dinner on the way home than buy groceries and cook them yourself. The rude awakening is when you realize those "pick up dinners" add up to more than you budgeted for groceries. That leads me to this question: Is your laziness or lack of planning today causing issues for yourself later?

You may choose to rethink your habit of buying the latest trendy clothing or hitting the bars with friends every Friday. You may decide to change where or how often you travel or even the type of car you buy. If your vacation plans revolve around beaches, is the sand and sun really that much better in another country than it is somewhere that you can drive? The answers to all of these questions will help you align your current lifestyle with the one you want in the future. I give you this Les Brown quote again to help you change: "Do what is easy, and your life will be hard. Do what is hard, and your life will become easy." Let's make sure we are choosing to do the hard stuff today so we can be where we want to be in the future.

Sure, it's nice to have a luxury vehicle, but what if you could have less debt and more money to invest while driving a nice, non-luxury vehicle? I'm not saying to stop dreaming big. I'm just saying if your vision is to have great wealth, you might want to cut back on your current spending to get there faster.

I'm not recommending going from where you are today to living the austere life of a monk. If I were a single guy, I might go that far to get a jump on my future wealth, but most of us have other people in our lives, and relationships cost money. You might really need that bigger place to live, the utilities it takes to run it, a car that seats six instead of five, a hefty grocery bill, sports fees, and a clothing budget because kids grow. I get it. I'm living that life myself. What I'm getting at is to be proactive about deciding how to best *use* your money rather than letting your lifestyle rule your money.

Here's a personal example: I have chosen to drive new vehicles only. They save me the time required to deal with the breakdowns and maintenance that come with older vehicles. On the other hand, I have never spent more than $55,000 on a new car. There were times when I wanted to but didn't. I decided to take the extra $30,000-plus I could have spent on a much nicer vehicle and instead used that money to advance my wealth journey. The lesson here is that a new car under $55,000 will get me 80 percent of what I want and need. The additional $30,000 for that extra luxury will only get me an additional 10 percent of what I want. Not much juice for the squeeze. On the other hand, investing that $30,000 into my vision could increase my odds of achieving the wealth I want.

I personally look at every dollar as a possible dollar invested in my overall vision. There's a purpose for every dollar, whether it's $500 or $50,000. I may place the money in my savings account. I may pay down a credit card, car loan, or even buy an index fund. If I gained access to an extra $10,000 right now, I might finish funding my IRA. With enough cash, I might make a down payment on a rental property. Being someone who invests heavily in my education, I might seek out a new educational opportunity with the money I didn't spend on a more luxurious vehicle. As you can see, I have decided that the money I could spend on a higher-end vehicle will better serve me somewhere else, and I am conscious of that decision.

Remember, I'm a utilitarian kind of guy. I do not enjoy retail therapy like some; it actually gives me anxiety. I get a rush from investing money rather than spending it. I understand that not many people are like me. Yet there are also not many people who have risen from collecting welfare to wealth in twelve years. Hopefully, your starting point is not as low as mine. I had to make some drastic changes. In your situation, maybe some relatively minor changes will accelerate your wealth achievement.

If you had neglected to review your spending for quite some time, you probably found several expenses that are unnecessary today. When you eliminate them, enjoy that feeling for a few moments. If you previously had a sense of being in a financial squeeze, it'll be like taking a deep breath of fresh air. It's the feeling of getting free money. It's not really free, but the feeling is the same. It's one degree closer to your vision.

Eliminate enough of the waste, and it will be like giving yourself a raise. The entire purpose of this book is for you to start redirecting some of your "spent" money so it can earn money for you instead of going into The Black Hole, never to be seen again! That's the path to real wealth.

CHAPTER 5

Wealth Tracker

WHEN I WAS a young teen, I played a text-based online video game. There were no cool graphics like today's games, only letters and numbers. In that game, players would travel the world defeating non-player characters (NPCs), gaining levels, building inventory, and collecting gold. You could also attack other players if you cared to create enemies.

I don't know why it intrigued me so much, but I became really good at it. I couldn't tell you if there were one hundred players in the game or five thousand, but I became the best at building wealth. What I figured out was that a single player could only hold so much inventory. So, I created another character I could control, and he would act as an additional space to keep weapons and armor. I actually named him Storage. His only job was to collect my winnings and hold them, almost like a bank. I would then work on selling the items from that cache. I ended up having so much money in the game that the interest paid to me was too much for the system, and I crashed the financial system. It would be the same if one individual in the world had $30 trillion.

Thinking back on that experience, I realize it was my ability to strategize and maneuver that allowed me to be so successful. My strengths in identifying, organizing, and prioritizing my assets and actions allowed me to play more efficiently than anyone else. Fortunately for me, and now you, I have translated those skills to the game of wealth. We don't have to be financial geniuses to win. We just need to observe the situation so we can get organized and create a plan to improve.

Some of my clients have balked, at first, at identifying what was wrong with their wealth plans. That's because they already knew what the problem was. Their views about and lack of skills in money management were the problem. They were forced to come to grips with the sometimes-harsh reality that they were where they were financially because of decisions *they* made and actions *they* took. They had a hard time admitting accountability. Maturity is when you stop complaining and making excuses for your life. You realize it's time to start making new choices to change your life for the better.

The Starting Point

Before we can make improvements that will get us where we want to be, we need to take stock of where we are starting. It's time to get all of your financial information in one place. Now, this might be quite challenging at first. Your information might be scattered all over. You might not even know where this information lies, but I know it can be found.

We're going to work together to create two essential documents: a Debt Sheet and a Net Worth Sheet. The Debt Sheet is nothing more than a list of all the money you owe to others. The Net Worth Sheet is where you determine the difference between the value of what you own and your debt. These are two tools that will help you recognize where you are today. We will also use them to determine a strategy for achieving your future goals.

Remember the chapter on awareness when I talked about neglect? If you don't like numbers, you might put off creating those documents. I get it. In my case, I've always been good with numbers but not so good with letters. Don't ask me to spell anything. Don't look too closely at my handwriting. Even though I know the content of this book so well, I saw the writing of it as a daunting task. I put it off for nearly two years after I was first advised to write it. I didn't know how to go about it. I didn't know where to find the information needed to create a plan to get it done. If this is where you're at, producing the numbers needed for this chapter, it's okay. I'll help you pull it all together.

The Debt Sheet

Hopefully, you realize that debt does not equal wealth in most cases. You'd be surprised to learn that some people equate wealth with owning a lot of things that are not really assets. What they own is for show, but it's a façade that's hiding massive bad debt. There is such a thing as positive debt, which is used to finance assets that work for you, but it can be hard to manage. It's vital to take extreme care and gain the knowledge necessary to handle it properly. Good debt can turn into bad debt if handled incorrectly. Overall, eliminating all debt should be your focus.

We are going to focus on any debt you may have and come up with a plan to eliminate it. It is unlikely that this will happen quickly unless your debts are small. By small, I mean less than a few thousand dollars.

For your Debt Sheet, you will need a list of all of your liabilities, or money you owe others, and the details about each one. Open a spreadsheet or grab a pad of paper and add the information from the list below in separate columns.

1. The name of each institution or person you owe money to. This includes your mortgage company, the finance company for your car loan, each credit card, taxes, and any money you may owe to a family member or friend.
2. The account number for each debt. This sheet will become an important reference for you, so adding the account number will save you time in the future.
3. The principal balance
4. The monthly payment
5. The interest rate
6. The date you opened the account
7. The initial loan amount
8. The maturity date. If you make all the scheduled payments, not a penny more, when will this debt be paid in full? We will compare this to your goal of being debt-free. If this date is beyond your goal, we know we will want to come up with a strategy to accelerate the payoff.

9. Rate change frequency, if any
10. The date of any rate change frequency, if any

Once you have filled in all the blanks with this information, take a deep breath. If you have a lot of debt, seeing it all in one place can be overwhelming. This step is like setting up the board for a game of chess. All we are doing is preparing. No strategy is involved yet. There's no need for fear. We are just lining up the pieces that we will use to develop a strategy.

Pause with me here for a moment and think. Doesn't it make sense that you should already have a total list of your debts somewhere? Doesn't this seem like the responsible thing to do? Isn't this something you would recommend to a family member or friend? If you agree with me, recognize that doing this work is something positive. It's a step toward getting your financial house in order.

The Net Worth Sheet

If you have never done this before, please understand that this is a score sheet for how you are doing. If you don't like what you see, that's okay. Let that disappointment be your motivation to change. As you pay off your debt and increase your assets, it will become fun to watch the numbers change to your benefit. You'll be able to track your progress and increase your confidence in your ability to achieve the wealth you envisioned in Chapter 2.

Since simplicity is one of the keys to wealth, if you are using a spreadsheet, I want you to create your Net Worth Sheet in the same document as your Debt Sheet. Simply add a second sheet within the document. By the way, we want to title this document "Wealth Tracker." Sheet 1 should be named "Debts," and Sheet 2 should be named "Net Worth." If you are confused about how to set this up, ask someone who is more familiar with spreadsheets, or Google it. It's a valuable skill to have.

As we continue through the Cheviron Pyramid of Wealth, you will update the information on these sheets often. They will provide a great visual representation of your progress on your journey. Personally, I like to update these sheets every three to six months or whenever there's a significant financial change in my life, such as paying off one of my debts.

Put the current date at the top of the document. You will want to add the date each time you update this sheet. It will help you track your progress and the amount of time it takes to get there.

Next, we'll list your assets. This will include only the larger items in your life, not your clothing, sports equipment, or hobby supplies. Let's say that we will only list items with a value greater than $1,000. The thinking here is, "If I sold off these assets, how much money would I have if I decided to retire and go live on an island for the rest of my life?" I call it my "island money." Am I taking $1,000 with me? Am I taking $50,000 or $5 million?

Here's a list of what to add to your Net Worth sheet:

1. Cash in the bank or readily at hand
2. Stock or mutual fund name and its current value
3. Real estate address(es) and value(s)

4. Crypto value
5. Gold, silver, or other precious metals' values
6. Whole life insurance policy value
7. Value of items such as artwork, jewelry, antiques, vehicles
8. IOUs, if anyone owes you money
9. Other items valued at over $1,000. This might include cars, boats, planes, or motorcycles.

Once you have listed your assets, total up their value. Next, retrieve the number from your Debt Sheet and transfer it to your Net Worth Sheet. Your debt, after all, is one of the elements of your Net Worth. Subtract the debt from your assets to get your net worth figure.

Never assume you are the only person who can answer questions about your assets. Invest the time now, when you first create your Wealth Tracker, to add the location or contact information for all the assets listed. If you get hit by the figurative bus tomorrow, you will want your loved ones to have easy access to all this information. Even better, if that bus misses you, you will have all the information about your assets in one place. If information about any of your assets needs to be reviewed in greater depth, you'll have your starting point at your fingertips. With your Wealth Tracker, you have now created a scoreboard showing how well you are doing toward achieving your wealth plan.

CHAPTER 6

Credit Score

THE WORK WE have done so far has been pretty heavy. If you've done the work requested in the previous chapters, I congratulate you. You should be feeling a sense of accomplishment. If you haven't completed it yet, go back to it after reading this chapter. You will need the results of that work to continue the journey of this book. The order of the chapters was designed specifically to alternate between heavy lifting and education. In this chapter, I give you a little breather in the exercises.

Let me begin by sharing that I'm not a credit score expert. I'm just a guy who, at a young age, didn't understand what a credit score was other than it was something I needed to pay attention to, and that a high number was better than a low one. So, I found ways to get there. Today, I am proud to say my score is in the Excellent range. I learned a lot of lessons along the way, and I plan to share them with you.

What is a Credit Score, and Why Should You Care About It?

According to EQUIFAX®, one of the three major credit bureaus that collects and analyzes personal financial information, a credit score is a three-digit number designed to represent the likelihood you will pay your bills on time. Your credit score tells lenders how much of a risk they may take if they lend you money. The higher your score, generally, the more favorable credit terms you will be able to get when requesting a loan. So, your score impacts not only whether you can get a loan, but also the interest rate and other terms.

Here's an example: When I went to get my last car loan as someone who has a high credit score, the interest rate I was offered was somewhere between 2 and 3 percent. When my nephew, who has a much lower credit score, requested a car loan, the best interest rate he could get was in the mid-teens. His loan payment is $200 more per month than it would be if he had my credit score. For someone in their early twenties, $200 per month can make a big difference in their lifestyle! Look back at your twenties. What could investing $200 a month have done for your wealth journey? My guess is that it would have made a big difference. After investing $200 monthly for six years at a 7 percent annual interest rate compounded monthly, you would have approximately $17,936.21. That's what I'm talking about!

A fact that surprises many people is that their credit rating can also affect their car insurance premiums. Many insurance companies use credit-based insurance scores to determine rates. Landlords also look at credit scores as part of their screening process for new tenants. They don't like renting to people who have low scores. Low scores equal high risk. Your credit score also impacts your ability to get credit cards and the interest rates the card companies charge.

The same concept applies to home loans. I have helped clients buy and sell a lot of homes over the years. Sadly, many of my clients, who wanted to buy a home, could not qualify for a loan because of their credit scores. They had to fix their scores first. Often, the delay caused them to have to spend more for their homes as home values increased. The point I'm trying to make is that one small thing, such as a poor credit score, can have a major impact on your life. You must become well-rounded on your wealth journey if you are going to make it.

Low Scores = Slow Progress

Think of your credit score as the brakes on your wealth vehicle. The lower your score, the more the brakes are applied, the longer your journey will take. The ultimate goal is to have no brakes on your wealth journey. You want to go as fast as you reasonably can.

I have yet to meet anyone whose vision is to achieve wealth by age ninety. Take that statement into full consideration when thinking about your journey. Most people think about how much money they need or want, but they don't understand the effect of time. I believe time has a greater impact on your wealth journey than money.

Credit Reporting Agencies

There are three major credit reporting agencies used by most lenders. They are Experian™, TransUnion®, and Equifax®. Each agency operates differently, so your score will likely vary by a few points with each. Potential lenders are likely to pull your numbers from all three agencies. They will use a formula based on those numbers to evaluate your creditworthiness.

My advice is to pull your credit report from each agency at least once a year. It doesn't cost anything. Upon review, you may discover that either your information is accurate, and you become very aware of what is reported, or you may find incorrect information that needs to be corrected. Maybe you'll see that you are on the cusp of achieving a higher score and now know how to act before requesting a new loan or applying for a new credit card.

The Numbers

Let's look at the numbers. Credit scores range from 300 to 850. The scores are broken into categories: Poor, Fair, Good, Very Good, and Excellent. I referred to the Experian credit bureau to get the number breakdown:

- Poor credit: 300–579
- Fair credit: 580–669
- Good credit: 670–739
- Very Good credit: 740–799
- Excellent credit: 800–850

If your score falls in the Fair range or below, you have a lot of work to do before moving forward on your wealth journey. A score like that tells lenders that you're not a reliable client to work with. It doesn't necessarily mean you will not pay it back. It may just mean you've had some issues or are new at establishing your credit. The bottom line is that you're less credible in the eyes of the lenders. When you achieve a rating in the Good range, you're more likely to be able to borrow money, but you may have a higher interest rate than someone with Very Good or Excellent credit. At the very minimum, I want you to work toward a score of 750 or greater, with the eventual goal of getting your score over 800.

What Counts Toward a Good Credit Score, and What Will Hurt?

The factors that affect your credit score positively are the following:

- Having your credit established for a long time. Generally, having a positive credit history for at least seven years is considered good. Having a positive history of ten to fifteen years will be more favorably viewed by most lenders.
- Your payment history. This means you've been making your payments on time.
- A good credit utilization ratio. This means the amount of debt you owe isn't a high percentage of your total available credit.
- Having a mix of credit types. This might include credit cards, retail accounts, installment loans (such as a car loan), and mortgage(s).

Then, it just makes sense that the negative factors include:

- Having little or no credit history
- Failing to pay your bills on time
- Having too many recent applications for credit
- Having a high amount of credit available as it relates to your income
- Having unpaid bills that go to collections. This may include loans, credit card debts, medical bills, utility bills, and government debts, for example.
- Closing a credit card account
- Allowing a foreclosure or repossession

When it comes to having a Very Good or Excellent credit score, the goal is to be proactive about the positive contributing factors and avoid the negative ones.

Regarding the length of an established credit account, I personally have a card that I will never close. I've had it for over eighteen years. I don't use it much anymore, but I understand the value of having a long credit history.

Here's an example of what to consider regarding your credit usage: Let's say you have a credit card with $1,000 of available credit. If you use that whole amount and keep that card "maxed out," your credit score will go down. If you have a $10,000 limit on that card, and you only use $1,000 of it, your score is likely to increase as long as you pay at least the minimum amount on time. By using only 10 percent of the limit, you are being a wise steward of your available credit.

Early Stages of Establishing Credit

Before opening any type of credit-building account or getting a credit card, I highly recommend checking your credit score with all three reporting bureaus. Doing this allows you to check whether someone has gained access to your personal information. You want to ensure there are no fraudulent accounts already established in your name. If you find something attributed to you that's not yours, the agencies have a process for you to request its removal. When you reach out to them with a request to dispute their information, creditors have thirty days to investigate and notify you of their findings. This is likely to result in a correction to your report. Once you know your report is clean, take slow steps toward establishing your credit.

The first method I used to establish my credit was with a credit builder account. Remember my truck accident? I used the insurance payment from the accident with my truck for this. You are likely to find this type of account available at smaller banks or through a credit union. It is especially helpful for people with no or low credit scores.

Then, *deposit your own money* into a credit-builder savings account. This account is securely held by the bank. You do not access the funds immediately. You make an arrangement with the bank to pay a specific amount into the account for a period of time. Your monthly payments are reported to the credit bureaus. At the end of the plan, you have access to the money minus any fees.

There is also something called a credit-builder loan. This gives you access to a small loan amount. This might be as little as $300 or as much as $1,000, and loan terms typically range from six to twenty-four months. Credit-builder loans function in the opposite manner of typical personal loans. Instead of getting funds upfront in a lump sum, you make payments each month and receive your balance at the end of the loan term. Here's how it works:

- The lender sets aside its money in a savings account for you. It's considered a loan by credit reporting agencies.
- You make payments toward the amount each month.
- You build credit over time. Credit-builder lenders typically report your payment history to the credit bureaus, helping you strengthen your credit with on-time monthly payments.
- At the end of the loan term, after you've made all the agreed-upon payments, you gain full access to the money.
- You'll typically pay interest on this account, but the lender may return a portion of that paid interest or the interest earned on the account to you at the end of the loan term.

Another "secured" option for establishing credit is a secured credit card. Secured credit cards require a cash deposit—usually equal to your credit limit—to be made when you open the account. This money acts as collateral every time you make a purchase. If you fail to make payments on time or default on your debt, your lender can use the deposit to reimburse itself.

Secured credit cards work similarly to debit cards in that you're using your own money as insurance for transactions, rather than borrowing funds from a lender. However, unlike a debit card, the payment history for your secured card may be reported to the three nationwide consumer reporting agencies.

Another way to initially establish your credit score is to open a credit card as soon as you turn eighteen. Be aware that some issuers require cosigners for applicants under the age of twenty-one. To be eligible at eighteen, you must be able to show you have enough income to repay the card limit. Getting a card at a young age can be a double-edged sword. One, you can get that credit card and go into debt really fast. Two, you learn to use credit well. My suggestion is to open a card with a small limit, say $1,000 or less. Then, exercise discipline to charge only one purchase on it each month, and when the bill comes, pay it in full immediately. The purpose of the card is *only* to establish your credit score, not to go into debt.

Even a $5 purchase will count toward using the card. When you pay it off, you will get a plus on your credit rating. Now, it doesn't matter if that purchase was for $5 or $500; you only get a single plus for making your payment on time. Be cautious about spending more than you can pay each month or getting caught in a cycle of paying only the minimum, especially when you are starting out. What really matters to the credit scoring agencies is that you are making a purchase and making an on-time payment. So why not build your credit with the lowest amount of money possible?

Raising Your Score

If your credit score is below the Good range, you have work to do. My first recommendation is to speak with a mortgage lender to get advice on specific steps to improve your score. Most of the lenders I've worked with are happy to offer this type of advice in the hope that you will become a client of theirs once your score is high enough. Of course, you can find a lot of information online about steps to take to improve your score, but I like creating those personal connections.

You might also consider working with a credit repair specialist. These are people or businesses that do the work for you by finding mistakes in your credit report and disputing them on your behalf. There is a fee for this service, so you will have to weigh the cost against investing your time doing this work. Personally, I have a hard time paying someone to do something just because I don't understand it. I'd much rather invest my time learning how to fix it and prevent it from happening again.

If your score is low due to habits like having a high credit limit, maxing out cards, being late with payments, or paying less than the minimum amount, only you can fix that. A credit repair specialist can't do that. You can use the positive habits I teach in Chapter 11 to help with this.

Having too much credit available compared to your income can be detrimental. Closing a credit card completely will temporarily lower your credit score. Reducing your credit limit will likely do that as well, but it may be wise to do so with the card you've had the shortest amount of time. By lowering your available credit dollars with either method, your credit utilization ratio increases. In layman's terms, an increase in your credit utilization ratio means you're using a higher percentage of the credit you have available. If having less money available to spend will help you curb your spending, this might just be what needs to be done. Again, it will be a temporary negative hit on your score, but it may help your score in the long run.

As a final word on the impact of your credit score, if you are an entrepreneur, your credit score will affect your ability to get loans for your business. A low score might prevent another person from partnering with you or keep investors from providing money for growth and expansion. If you have a business partner and decide to buy them out, again, a low score could prevent you from getting the necessary loan.

EXERCISE:

Pull your credit score and study it. Dispute anything that is not correct. Find out what your current credit utilization score is, then build a plan to decrease it so you can increase your overall credit score.

____

____

____

____

____

____

CHAPTER 7

Simplify to Focus

IT IS TIME to realign with your vision from Chapter 2, keeping in mind what's really important to you according to your definition of wealth. The key factors we will focus on are your vision and goals; then, we will consider how much time you have left in life to achieve them.

When I work with clients struggling to achieve their vision of wealth, I find that using a jigsaw puzzle delivers a startling lesson. I pull out a box of four rather simple puzzles meant for toddlers. One puzzle has penguins on it, another has bears, the third puzzle has a lion, and the fourth has a monkey. Four different puzzles, all found in one box similar to this:

I also grab a timer. Note, I haven't shown them the picture on the box yet. That's how life is, isn't it? When you first start, you don't know how it will look.

I then say, "This puzzle is a representation of your life. When I say 'go,' I want you to dump out the pieces and start putting your puzzle together. I'm going to allow you fifteen seconds per decade you have remaining in life to complete it."

Now, none of us knows exactly how much time we have left in this world, so we use a national average life span. For men, typically, that's about seventy-five years of age. For women in the United States, it's eighty. What I'm trying to help them understand is that no matter how long we live, we are always running against a clock. Once we agree on the number of decades they have left, I set the timer and say "go." They dump out the puzzle pieces, spread them out, and turn them over.

I ask them how their "life," their puzzle, is looking at each fifteen-second interval. Most of the time, the answer I get is "It's a mess." It usually *is* a mess at that point. The timer continues. I say, "Hey, you're ten years older" every fifteen seconds and give them their specific age. Nearly every one of them has told me they start to feel pressure about completing the puzzle. This is the same pressure we feel as we age and realize we may not get where we want to go in the time we have left.

Most clients complete between two and three of the sections before the clock stops. The purpose of the exercise is to demonstrate how quickly time passes. Most often, this creates a sense of disappointment because the client isn't far enough along in their wealth journey yet. It may even create stress when they realize there isn't enough time to complete their puzzle. I want them to feel those feelings but not fall into despair about where they are on their life journey. So, I have them move on to the next step fairly quickly.

Here is where the magic happens. I ask them to do the puzzle a second time with the same amount of time. The only difference is that we simplify the exercise. I ask them to choose to complete only one of the four puzzles. Their choice is then compared to their life's vision.

Let's say they choose the penguin puzzle. I start the timer, and the client dumps out the puzzle. Focusing solely on the pieces that fit the penguin section of the puzzle, it comes together much faster. In fact, most do it in fifteen seconds or less, equating to a single decade. Interesting, isn't it? Having clarity of focus about their vision made all the difference. All the non-penguin puzzle pieces were just distractions. They were quickly ignored, even shoved aside, because they got in the way of achieving the goal of putting together the penguin picture.

The Power of Focus

My goal with this exercise is to help you and all of my clients understand the power of focus, the power of simplifying and eliminating all the distractions in life that are slowing your progress toward the achievement of wealth.

There's a noteworthy concept called shiny object syndrome. It's a tendency to get distracted by new ideas or opportunities irrelevant to your current plan or path. I get it. It's interesting and even fun to learn about new things. The critical questions to ask when you encounter them are these:

- Does this new idea or opportunity contribute in some way to my wealth journey?
- Does it allow me to move faster toward my vision, or does it steer me away from my current path?
- Is it even worth my time and attention?
- Was I looking for this new idea or opportunity prior to its arrival? Have I identified it as something I really need to move closer to the life I desire? Or did it just happen to come up, and I am now considering investing valuable time thinking about it?

I learned from the former publisher of *SUCCESS* magazine, Darren Hardy, that "if it is not a hell yes, then it's got to be a hell no." I have used that filter many times in my life, and it helps me reject shiny objects and get back on the path where I belong.

Those who fall prey to shiny object syndrome tend to be weak in their belief that they are on the correct path. They may have doubts about their ability to achieve their vision. Maybe they're not clear enough about their vision, so they do not quickly dismiss those shiny objects as unimportant.

Early in my wealth journey, I was prone to spending a lot of time evaluating nearly every opportunity that came my way. I was probably suffering from what's called a Fear of Missing Out (FOMO). I didn't understand the need to have a filter for opportunities. I thought every one of them deserved my attention.

One day, while waiting for a meeting about an opportunity, I opened the book *Failing Forward* by John Maxwell. The first thing my eyes landed on was a paragraph about getting off the failure freeway. It made me question what "freeway" I was on at that moment. When I opened the book, I had left off on Chapter 5: *Get Off the Failure Freeway*. My heart stopped when I read just the chapter title. I paused and asked myself, "What does this mean?" In that moment, I realized the opportunity I had been so heavily pursuing might not be an opportunity at all. It might be a distraction or something to take me off course from the growth I was pursuing. Without reading a single word beyond the title, I closed the book, ran upstairs to my office, where my father was sitting, and showed him what I had just seen. I shared my thoughts with him—how this might be a sign, a warning. I don't remember exactly what he said, but I'll never forget how he validated my feelings and confirmed what I was beginning to suspect: this might not be the opportunity I thought it was.

When I first read about the "Failure Freeway," I saw it a little differently than most. Typically, people associate it with something broken—a path that isn't working and needs to be abandoned. But I realized the Failure Freeway isn't always obvious. Sometimes, everything appears to be working fine—today. The systems are running, the results are showing up, and the road feels smooth. But the question is, "Does this road lead to where I want to go?"

If the answer is no, if it doesn't take you to your intended destination, then, by definition, it's going to fail you. That's the Failure Freeway. Not because it's broken now, but because it won't get you where you're trying to go later. And that kind of failure, the subtle kind, is often the costliest.

I ask myself this question regularly, "Is this road going to get me where I want to go?" If the answer is no, then I know I'm on the Failure Freeway. It might not feel like a problem today, but eventually, it will be. If I stay on this road too long, I'll reach the end with no way forward, and, at that point, I risk wrecking my metaphorical car trying to force my way through. That costs more time, money, and energy to recover than exiting earlier.

My pro tip? I routinely evaluate the roads I'm on—my habits, relationships, business models, routines—and ask, "Where does this actually take me?" If the destination doesn't align with my vision, I get off that freeway. I don't wait for it to crash. I choose to exit early. Allowing myself to shift has saved me more than I can measure.

I wasn't confident in the opportunity, but I continued to press forward. But, seeing that passage as I waited, I took that as a sign to walk away from that investment and focus my time elsewhere. Though it appeared to be a good opportunity, it just wasn't right *for me*. My "no" might have been a "hell, yes" to 99 percent of the world. However, saying no ended up being an incredible life-altering decision.

That experience caused me to start watching for "Failure Freeway" signs everywhere I went. I'm constantly asking if God is guiding me toward opportunities that apply to my wealth journey or away from ones that are nothing more than distractions. And you know what? The signs are all around me. I just wasn't aware of them before that early experience. I don't let those signs slip by anymore. My awareness is on high alert all the time.

Now, I ask you, what signs are you seeing that indicate whether certain opportunities will move you forward or backward on your wealth journey? If you've not seen signs yet, increase your focus on what you want, and they will appear.

Staying True to the Vision

After being around real estate agents for most of my formative years, I became one. Since I had young kids at the time, I had a vision for my life that included a lot of family time. I wanted to be home for dinner every night at 5:00 p.m. I wanted to be at the kids' school and sporting events. I refused to schedule appointments on Sundays. If you're not familiar with the life of the typical real estate agent, they tend to be on call nearly twenty-four-seven for their clients. I wasn't willing to sacrifice my personal life, so I came up with a schedule that worked for me. Then, I created systems that allowed me to finish everything that needed doing within that time frame. If a client only had Sunday or evenings to look at homes, I'd ask another agent for help who *would* work during those times.

I did well as an agent, and it took me a good distance on my wealth journey. To go further, the next step in that career would be to own a real estate office. Guess what? Taking on the responsibility of a real estate office would have run counter to my life's vision of having more time freedom. My life would have become much more complicated. Fortunately for me, the opportunity to own that company fell through. I was devastated at first because I had invested eight months of my life preparing for that transition. But you know what? I understood that opportunity wasn't meant to be part of my life's puzzle. It just wasn't going to help me achieve my vision.

I'm asking you to think about the vision you chose in Chapter 2. Think about your goals. Then, consider what is going on in your life right now that isn't contributing to their achievement. Look at all the pieces of your life.

- What relationships don't serve your progress toward that vision?
- What activities?
- What commitments do you currently have that might be pulling you off your path to wealth?

- What money are you spending, going back to your list from Chapter 4, that might have a better use?
- What steps can you take to simplify and stay focused on your journey's progress?

I ask myself those questions at least once every year. It's part of the evolution of my thinking, actions, and vision. I audit my relationships, my systems, my next steps, and everything I use, including my money, assets, and debts. There have been times when the person I evolved into changed my vision from what I thought I wanted the previous year. Each year, I move closer to the vision I have for my life, and as I do, my happiness and overall satisfaction continue to grow.

Simplifying your life is a constant evolution. You are becoming the person who has the wealth you desire. This is one area in which subtraction does not mean less. Subtracting the pieces of your life puzzle that don't serve your vision actually adds strength and speed to your journey.

I compare this level of focus to the Kevin Costner movie, *For the Love of the Game*. The main character is a baseball pitcher nearing the end of his career, and he hasn't been playing well. He's in his final game with 40,000 fans cheering. In the movie, he uses a technique that made him great, enabling him to block out everything except his next pitch. He referred to that technique as "silence the mechanism." I think of that phrase every time I feel the pull of distractions. I now silence the noise those distractions create, seeking to proactively simplify my life so I can remain highly focused on my wealth journey.

CHAPTER 8

Categorize

FOR THIS CHAPTER, pull out the spending sheet you created in Chapter 4 and categorize every item. As a "simplify" kind of guy, I'll have you limit the categories to three: Fixed, Lifestyle, and Extras. The goal is to create forward progress, not get mired in the details.

But before we do that, let's go over some of the potential challenges or obstacles you might encounter along the way. There is an emotional aspect when it comes to money. As we covered in Chapter 3, we all have feelings around our approach to spending, saving, and investing. When we have others in our lives to consider, such as a spouse, kids, or other loved ones, they have feelings about money, too. Their feelings need to be considered, because how they feel will, undoubtedly, affect our feelings about the analysis we do here.

I'm not saying other people's feelings need to be the same as yours, but if you're sharing your bucket of money with others, you all need to accept responsibility for your spending habits as they relate to your joint vision and goals for your life. In my case, I've mentioned how much of a saver I am. I do not enjoy spending money. It actually causes me anxiety and stress when my family spends money. Most of the time, I'd rather not be there when it happens.

I enjoy investing money as I see it as a tool to help me achieve my vision. My wife enjoys spending money. Now, you might think this causes friction in my household, and I'd be lying if I said it never happened. However, I have learned from my wife that it's important to balance my desire to save and invest with her desire for our family to enjoy a certain lifestyle and create memories with our kids. Understanding this balance in a relationship is the key to staying happily married. What I'm getting at is that you may need to be somewhat flexible in determining your categories of spending.

Seasons of Life

Now, there are seasons of life during which financial stability swings one way or the other. Early on, we were on welfare, and it was all about clipping coupons, only buying what was on sale, and waiting for Black Friday or another big discount day to make major purchases. We had to be uber conservative with our spending because there wasn't enough income to splurge, only enough to keep a roof over our heads and food on the table. Even though this season was hard, my long-standing desire to save money worked to our advantage. We made the choices and sacrifices necessary to keep ourselves afloat.

During our next season, when the amount of money flowing into our bucket increased, my wife and I made different decisions. When we were able to lessen our grip on expenses, my thinking revolved around these three questions:

1. How can we tighten the budget to have money to invest without negatively impacting our lifestyle?
2. How can I protect the money I'm earning?
3. How can I be a good steward of the money coming in?

The important message here is that you and your partner agree on what season you are in. If you believe you're in different seasons, there will likely be some conflicts. Some negotiations may be necessary to find a savings versus spending profile that is acceptable to both of you. If you choose to do life with someone else, it can't just be about you, or there is a high chance you will do life by yourself. And if this means a dissolution of marriage, I would guess you could end up with 40 percent of what you initially had. That is not a great wealth choice.

With money issues being one of the biggest causes of divorce, it's critical to get this right. If I remain in season one, wanting to cut costs to the bare minimum and clip coupons while my spouse lives in season two, where there is plenty of breathing room financially, we have disconnected. Before we start applying categories to expenses, we need to make some agreements around the current season. The questions to ask are these:

- What is our shared vision for where we want to be versus where we are today?

- How quickly do we want to get there?
- What can we do to take the next few steps toward our vision?
- If we tighten our spending for six months, are the sacrifices worth the gain? And, if so, where do we agree to make cuts?

Some strong feelings might come up during these conversations. You may have to refer back to Chapter 3 on your awareness around money versus the awareness your partner has. Acceptance of each other's point of view and experiences is important before making any changes.

Your Category Baselines

By knowing where the money is going and determining our baseline for each category, we can determine how much we need to come in every month to support our current lifestyle. Let's say the amount we are spending monthly is $10,000, and we're satisfied with our current lifestyle and progress toward our vision. As long as we have that $10,000 each month, we are doing great, and no immediate changes are required.

When we review our progress toward our vision, we may find that we are either ahead of schedule or behind. If we're behind, the spending analysis is useful for finding money to return to our chosen path to wealth. When expenses start to expand to where they're eating up all of the income, it's time for a spending analysis and possibly a reset of the budget so the Saving and Investing categories get fed as well as the Lifestyle and Extras categories. Before we get to that point, let's establish that baseline.

EXERCISE:

It's time to dig deeper into the work you did in Chapter 4 on spending. You want to get a clear picture of how some of your money works for you and how you're letting some of it work against you. The first step is to assign a category to every expense. Here's why:

- To determine where the money is going, especially money spent without a significant return
- To determine how much money is being invested into your future, going toward achieving your vision, versus how much is just being spent

We're going to separate each "spend" into one of three categories: Fixed, Lifestyle, and Extras. Your fixed expenses will be things like your mortgage or rent, utilities, groceries, and gas. Lifestyle choices might be a gym membership, sports fees for your kids, eating out, and vacation travel. Extras are items we spend money on that don't really fulfill us. In some cases, my clients have found that the Extras are greater than their Fixed and Lifestyle spending combined.

So, take a look at your Spending list. Separate the information by month and assign one of these three categories to each item. If you are unsure which category to use for an expense, move it to the next category. For example, if you're not sure if an expense should be categorized as Lifestyle, move it into Extras. If you're not sure if something is a Fixed expense, move it into Lifestyle. This will help keep you honest and give you an advantage when we come back to this subject later in this book.

You're bound to encounter items that could fit into more than one category. Let's use clothing as an example. Clothing, in general, is a necessity. That would make it a Fixed expense, especially if you have kids who are growing rapidly. When you choose designer clothing brands over less expensive ones, those clothes might fall into the Lifestyle category. If you purchase the same style of shoes in multiple colors, we might be looking at an expense for the Extras category. Don't stress over these decisions. Just choose your definition for each category as it fits with how you live your life today.

Let me give you an example from my personal life. My family loves going to Disney World. We go at least once a year. It's our primary vacation spot. My wife and kids enjoy the quality of the experience. I also enjoy the trip because I like to give my family experiences that they enjoy. And, for me, I appreciate the level of customer service Disney provides. I find the Disney experience to always be a learning opportunity. They get so many things right that they inspire me to innovate and improve my own business at every turn.

Let's break down our spending on one of these trips and how each expense fits into different categories. When you get this dialed in, you will recognize the difference between what can be lumped together and what should be broken down.

The first thing we do is book our plane tickets. We tried driving to Disney one year from our home in Northern Indiana. It wasn't a great experience for any of us. The plane tickets fall into the Lifestyle category. Sitting in any available open seat adds no additional charge, but we want to sit together, so we pay a little extra for four seats together. The "extra" for those seats could possibly be added to the Extras category.

In my opinion, we should be able to get all of our travel essentials, clothing, and the like, into two bags. My family disagrees. Each person wants to have their own bag. There's a fee for some of those bags. So, I put the cost of the first two bags in the Lifestyle category and the cost of the second two in Extras. The expense wasn't necessary other than to make my family members happy. Please know, if you save a dollar and your family hates you because of it, you are not really winning.

If I choose to have a drink on the flight, it goes into the Lifestyle category. If I decide the stress of traveling with my family calls for a second drink, that could be considered an Extra expense.

Next up is transportation in Orlando. I know that the majority of our time will be spent on the Disney property, so I vote to use Uber. The cost of Uber falls into Lifestyle. If we choose to get a rental car, I call that an Extra, though my wife might categorize it as a Lifestyle item. It's something we have to talk about and agree on during each trip. Who's to say either one of us is entirely right here?

What about the hotel? There are plenty of economical options throughout Orlando. However, we like to stay at Disney's The Port Orleans - Riverside. It's convenient, clean, and we've had good experiences there. The hotel room expense falls into the Lifestyle category. If we upgraded to a different property, the additional cost would fall into the Extras category. The same applies to a quick walk to get ice cream. Snacks are Extras in my line of thinking. Meals are part of Lifestyle. If we purchase the special Disney cups offered at breakfast, they might be considered Extra at first, but with those cups, you can get unlimited drinks on the property, so that's probably a wash, and I consider that a Lifestyle category.

The fee to get into the park goes under Lifestyle. The first thing our family does upon entering is look at the trading pins. One pin per person is an expected expense for each trip. That's Lifestyle. Any additional pins are Extras (according to me). It's the same for any souvenir or item of clothing. We brought plenty of clothing with us. We don't *need* clothing, so it's an Extra expense, unless you pull "an Austin" and completely forget to bring shorts to Florida. Then, it is a Lifestyle expense. I'm sure you get the picture.

Some of your spending will fall into more than one category, and only you (and perhaps your partner) can determine which one fits best. When you have an expense from somewhere like Amazon or Target, did the purchase include groceries, which is a Fixed expense? Or was it clothing that falls into the Lifestyle category? Maybe you purchased home maintenance items, which are another Fixed expense. For the initial exercise, when you come across charges from businesses like that, let's split them between Lifestyle and Extras. If you want to dig deeper to determine the best category to put them in, with online retailers, you can print out a list of your last ninety days of orders to help you break things down more accurately. For our immediate purposes, let's stay general with our category assignments.

This exercise takes time. It takes thought. It may get a little frustrating. Please stick with it. The first time you do this, you will be required to make judgments or evaluations. Once you make a few of those decisions, the rest becomes easier.

By doing this exercise, you'll find a baseline for each category of expenses. Later in the book, I'm going to help you find money to apply to the advancement of your wealth plan. Some of it may be found by adjusting in one category, or maybe in all three. So, finding your baseline will be important. Keep in mind that all of this work links back to achieving the vision you have for your life as quickly as possible.

By doing this analysis, some of my clients identified some bad habits. Putting a dollar amount on those bad habits was a rude awakening, as they already knew of better ways to use that amount of money. Once they saw where it had been going, their desire for the "better way" made it easy to change their spending habits. The focus became one of having money work for their future, not just consuming it all today.

An item to make a judgment call on might be your car payment. Unless you live in a big city with an excellent transportation system, having a vehicle is probably a necessity. That puts your car payment and vehicle insurance in the Fixed category. The question arises with the type of vehicle you choose to drive. If you're driving a Lamborghini, that vehicle, or at least a portion of its expense, probably falls into the Lifestyle or Extras category.

When considering subscription services such as Netflix or Apple TV, some may consider them a Fixed expense. Others may see those subscriptions as Lifestyle or even Extras. The only correct answer here is what's right for you in your world.

When it comes to food, you're going to have grocery expenses that are considered Fixed. If you're like most people, you will have picked up or gone out for food during the ninety-day period we are examining. So, you might have spent money at McDonald's, Starbucks, Chipotle (like me), your favorite pizza place, or another restaurant. Some of those purchases might fall into Lifestyle, others into Extras. If you have only made purchases in those places once a month, you might consider those Lifestyle purchases. The third or fourth purchase at any of those places will likely fall into the Extras category. After all, you did buy groceries, probably with the intent to prepare some meals at home.

The goal is to get a bird's-eye view of how much of your money is spent in each category. We'll go deeper into each category later in the book. The main point is to find where your money is going right now. If there is more being spent on Lifestyle than Extras, there's no judgment. If your most significant spend is on Extras and you are happy and comfortable with how you are living your life, so be it. The point is that when you treat $1 with the same respect you treat $1,000, you are more likely to do the hard work needed to start managing your money wisely.

CHAPTER 9

Debt

DEBT REDUCTION IS the eighth building block in the foundation of our wealth pyramid. I am a dedicated student of wealth and success. I read all the books. I attend events presented by incredibly knowledgeable speakers. I take notes on all of it. I try to learn something from every conversation I have, whether it's with an expert or someone I sit next to in the audience. I'm a fanboy of people like Robert Kiyosaki on one end of the spectrum and Dave Ramsey on the other. Robert Kiyosaki is best known as the author of *Rich Dad Poor Dad* and is an entrepreneur and investor who teaches people how to build wealth through financial education and strategic investing. Dave Ramsey, on the other hand, is a nationally syndicated radio host and author of *The Total Money Makeover*, known for helping millions of people get out of debt and take control of their finances. He strongly advocates for eliminating all debt and living a cash-based lifestyle. While their philosophies are vastly different, I've learned valuable lessons from both men.

I am also a huge fan of Dewitt Jones. He is a professional photographer for National Geographic. He also writes, directs films, and does public speaking. I had the privilege of hearing him speak in 2021. It was the best keynote presentation I've ever heard. A single sentence he spoke changed my entire paradigm. It was this: "There's more than one right answer."

You see, I had been searching for THE answer to building wealth, assuming there was one and only one. What I realized, after some thought, was that the only correct answer is what's right for me. I subscribe to some of what Dave Ramsey suggests regarding bad debt. I also subscribe to some of what Robert Kiyosaki teaches about using Other People's Money (OPM) to build wealth. For me, both have correct answers. I have integrated some of the strategies from each to build what's right for my personal journey toward wealth. I believe you'll find the same to be true for you. Rather than subscribing to one single method, it's essential to analyze how the information we gather applies to the vision we have for our lives. Investigate new ideas, then consider whether they make sense for you.

Debt Control = Freedom

I like to compare debt to fire. We have a gas fireplace in our home. It has a pilot light. The pilot light does no harm. It allows the fire to come to life when we want it. When the fire is lit, it is useful as well. It warms the room. It creates a nice ambience. Now, if that fire were to get out of hand, it could burn my whole house down. So, we take measures to keep it contained. I look at debt the same way. It is useful only when properly managed.

On a trip to Las Vegas for a convention, I had an interesting conversation with a taxi driver named Brandon. For some reason, we got talking about money. Brandon said something very profound: "When you get out of debt, you can do whatever you want." That's the best quote ever relating to bad debt. Always wanting to give credit where credit is due, I asked permission to quote him, and he agreed. I know exactly the feeling he was talking about. When debt is gone, it's like having a weight removed. The commitments that tied you to that debt likely prevented you from doing other things with your time and ~~your~~ money. With no debt, "you can do whatever you want."

You Are . . . Where?
What *Are* Your Current Debts?

I've found that, for most of us, the initial pile of debt we take on is usually bad debt. Now, it might be doing good things for us, such as providing for some important life expenses, like having a place to live or providing a vehicle. Do you know what your total debt is right now as you read this book? If you have been doing the exercises, you should be able to locate the number on your Wealth Tracker. Once you have that number, think about how you feel about it. What is it in relation to the amount of income you have? Is it smaller? Or, like most, is it larger than your annual income? If you own a home, that number is likely much larger than your annual income due to your mortgage. Does your number give you anxiety? Do you feel positive about it? If you've already been on a debt reduction journey, you might feel pretty good about the progress you've already made.

Next, add up your monthly debt payments. How much of your hard-earned money are you paying back to lenders? Once those debts are paid off, that amount will be extra money that you can use to fuel your vision, to move you farther along the path to wealth. That thought alone should be a tremendous motivator to learn what next steps you can take to reduce your debt.

Looking over your debt sheet, what's the highest interest rate you are paying a lender, whether it's a banking institution, a private lender, or a friend? Put a red star next to it on your sheet. That is possibly the debt we will tackle first. I say "possibly" because I also want you to identify the smallest debt you owe. If they are one and the same, great. If not, we may have to do some analysis.

When I look at debt reduction, I typically look at eliminating the debt with the highest interest rate first. I see that as the biggest hole in my financial boat. By plugging the biggest hole in the boat first, I slow the leak and regain control sooner. It is not just about paying off debt. It is also about stopping the most expensive losses first so that I can move forward with greater momentum.

However, if your lowest balance is not all that much, paying it off will create momentum. If your biggest debt also has the highest interest rate, you won't see dramatic results by chipping away at it first.

You must also consider time frames when planning for debt reduction. If you have a personal loan from a friend, relative, or even a bank that has a payoff deadline, it may be that that debt needs to be addressed first.

The goal with debt reduction is to get the biggest win possible in the shortest amount of time, whether the win is financial or emotional. Maybe that debt to the relative has been weighing on you emotionally, and you want it to be gone. Only you can decide where to begin. Personal and business debt typically fall into three categories:

1. Revolving credit card balances
2. Installment loans from banks (personal, auto, or student loans)
3. Money borrowed from family and friends

Where Can Debt Live in Your Life?

The path I chose to wealth involves owning rental real estate. At one point, I was able to purchase rentals properties using mortgage rates around 4 percent, while these properties earned returns around 20 percent. This meant that my mortgage debt was effectively netting me a 16 percent return. I consider that "good debt." However, it is important to emphasize that not all debt is worth the effort.

If I had to borrow at 4 percent just to earn anywhere between 4 to 8 percent, the juice simply wouldn't be worth the squeeze. I always consider the value of my time, energy, and risk tolerance before committing to a deal with such a narrow return. I've learned that sometimes saying no to an investment can accelerate my wealth journey even more than saying yes.

Another potential source of good debt is a line of credit. Please note the word "potential" here. A line of credit is only good debt when used to generate a return or carry you through an unexpected rough patch.

My rough patch, for me, occurred in 2022. As I was talking on the phone one day at my son's baseball game, I realized my words weren't coming out right. I ended the call with an apology and sat down. I began sweating profusely. I decided to just go home and go to bed.

When I woke up the next day, my speech was slow. My movement was slow. I knew something was terribly wrong, so I went to the emergency room. During the next eight hours, the doctors ran every test they could think of, and guess what? They found nothing wrong. In fact, the doctor even said my test results were those of a "thoroughbred." Everything checked out perfectly. What the heck? Something *was* wrong. My body wasn't functioning as I expected, as I needed it to.

I was fortunate to have a very direct nurse speak with me after the doctor delivered his results. She said, "Austin, you have too much stress in your life." I didn't want to believe her, as I had spent much of the previous four years reducing stressors in my life. I had stopped selling real estate to eliminate the weekly hassles involved with negotiations, appraisals, inspections, demanding clients, and closings. I pushed back against her assessment, but she wouldn't give up. She asked how many businesses I owned. At that time, it was eight. I mentioned owning rental properties. She asked how many.

It was forty single-family homes. I didn't feel that any of that caused me stress because those companies and houses were fast-tracking me to my vision of wealth. If anything, I saw them as "good stress." However, the bigger question became this: Were those businesses and rental properties also fast-tracking me into poor health?

I had no choice but to reflect on what I had built, what I had committed to, and to slow down. The recommendation was that I not work for two months. Two months! And what would happen if I didn't? The answer was that I might become incapacitated or even die. Well, getting rich and sick is stupid. That I understood. Right there in the hospital, I realized I had to reach a point of acceptance. I had to take the medical professionals' advice and make some major changes. And it was hard. Really hard. I'm not usually an emotional guy, but this hit me so hard that I cried over what I had to give up. I remember telling myself, "It was a good ride. You did well with what time you had." I was sad and a little scared about what would happen to my vision, but of course, my health was way more important.

So, how does this play into our conversation about debt? I did what I was told to do. I stopped working. There was a lot less money coming in during those two months. I needed time to figure out my next steps. I wasn't prepared to lay anyone off. Having a business line of credit allowed me to continue to make payroll for all my employees. The debt from the business line of credit kept me alive, mentally and emotionally, until I could revise my vision of my business life to improve my physical health.

What you and I don't want in our lives is bad debt. This would include credit card debt for anything that didn't generate a return or help us take a step toward our vision. This is where most people get into trouble. They use credit cards to provide instant gratification rather than seeking ways to use their money to make money. They then become, as the Bible says, "slave to the lender." They have committed future income to the repayment of that debt.

Understanding Credit Card Debt

Let's talk about that credit card debt. There are ways to accelerate its elimination. Let's say you have three credit cards. One might have $5,000 on it, another might have $10,000 on it, and the third might have been used for a considerable expense and have $20,000 on it. If you're paying 28 percent interest on them, that's around $700 per month that just goes toward the interest, not toward paying down the principal. A simple strategy to use that $700 against the principal would be to get a zero percent credit card and transfer your balances to it. This is possible with a credit score, at least, in the Good range. To find these offers, start by looking at credit card comparison websites or use AI to quickly tell you where to search. If technology is not your thing, you can always check with your local bank.

Now, most zero percent offers are only good for twelve or twenty-four months, so they won't help you pay off the whole amount, but you can certainly make a big dent in that bad debt by making the same payments with zero interest. If you put this strategy into action, in twelve months, you could pay down $8,400 of your balance or about 25 percent. See, thinking smarter and innovating ways to pay down your bad debt is what to strive for.

If you decide to use this strategy, be aware that when your zero percent interest period ends, any remaining balance begins to accrue interest at the card's regular APR, which is often much higher. Typically, it is so high that you could be heading backwards on your wealth journey. It is best to have a backup plan if the debt is not eliminated during the zero percent offer period.

There are other benefits to doing this as well. You no longer receive three statements. You no longer have three places to log in for information. You no longer have to be concerned about the potential for three cards getting hacked. You've applied the strategy from Chapter 7 to your debt. You have simplified your debt and focused on its elimination.

Beware of canceling those three other cards in this example. Each closure puts a dent in your credit score, as we learned in Chapter 6. Just set them aside or lock them in a safe for now so you don't use them for a while. Look up which you have had the longest and take note of that. That is the one you will want to keep for sure. You may eventually want to cancel the others, but not both at the same time. Consider canceling the newest card. Take the temporary hit to your credit score. When your score recovers, consider canceling the next newest card. Always, always keep the oldest card you have.

Like anything else that's important to your vision, effectively reducing debt requires you to plan out a strategy. I've covered the education I've gained that supports my vision. You may need additional education specific to your situation. Don't balk at it. Schedule it! Meet with a financial advisor or lender to determine the best way forward for you.

CHAPTER 10

Extras

IN THIS BUILDING block, Extras, I'm going to ask you to change how you're handling your money, but not necessarily your lifestyle. Remember, those are two separate categories. Keep your vision in mind when considering any expense in the Extras category. The emotions attached to your vision will make it easier to make changes. Be cautious, though, that when you get caught up in the emotions around how the money in that category was already spent, you'll do nothing more than hold yourself back.

If you balk at cutting things out of this category, you're probably going to be at the same place next year as you are today. You have made it this far in the book because you don't want that, right? You don't even want to be in the same place next month that you are today. Do you agree with me? Are you in? Are you ready to make some hard choices that could make your life easier? In actuality, the Extras category is where to find the biggest surplus with the least amount of pain.

Understand that there is a cost associated with your vision, and you are the only one who can decide how to fund it. Having an inspiring vision should generate enough motivation for you to want to make changes. Before we move into this exercise, take a good look at the vision you outlined in Chapter 2. Now is the time to find the funds for it. Let's get started!

Finding Money

In Chapter 8, we categorized our expenses. They fell into one of three areas: Fixed, Lifestyle, and Extras. For now, we are going to focus solely on our spending in the Extras category. Add up your total Extra expenses for the full three months you outlined. Then, divide that number by three to get the average amount you spend on Extras each month. As we covered, no two months of spending will be the same. There will be some higher and some lower. We want to work with the average. Next, multiply your monthly average spending on Extras by 25 percent. The formula looks like this:

Average Monthly Extras x 0.25 = Target Amount to Reduce

This is the amount you are going to commit to reducing your Extras spending by the end of the next ninety days. You may think that's too big a commitment to drop your Extras spending by 25 percent. After doing this exercise myself and with many clients, we have all been pleasantly surprised at how easy it can actually be once we dig into where the money has been going.

As an example, if the average amount in your Extras category is $4,000, your goal is to reduce that number to $3,000 a month, ninety days from now. ($4,000 x .25 = $1,000, $4,000-$1,000 = $3,000) I'm not asking you to drop your spending in this category by 25 percent in a single month, though some of my clients have found it to be very doable. You might even be able to cut your spending by that much tomorrow. I'm giving you ninety days to get it done.

Some changes will take time. Maybe you have some subscriptions that require a thirty-day cancellation period. If you have shared funds and expenses with a spouse, you will likely need to have some conversations around what is feasible or reasonable to cut and make some commitments together. Those discussions take time as well.

With the achievement of your vision in mind, I want you, and your spouse if you have one, and possibly even your kids, to fill in the blank in this statement:

I can live without ...

____

____

____

Your answers might range from "energy drinks" to "Starbucks" to "fast food." If you're not comfortable eliminating some of these items completely, you may decide to filter those answers a bit by saying, "I can live without Starbucks every day" or "I can live without fast food more than once a week." It's your decision to make while reviewing where all that money is going for Extras. Maybe a trip to Starbucks once or twice a week would fulfill your craving for their coffee instead of habitually popping in there once a day or more because it's convenient.

You can look at this process in several ways:

- Which items will eliminate the greatest amount of money from this category?
- Which items are we not ready to eliminate?
- Which items are easy to eliminate?

Place a star next to any item in the Extras category that you and your spouse agree you can live without. Consciously work toward eliminating spending money on them for ninety days. Be aware that there may be some emotions tied to the items that get starred.

Sometimes, the Extras category expenses can be pared down with a bit of advance planning instead of being completely eliminated. For example, let's consider a last-minute weekend getaway. Did you have more fun or relaxation by staying three nights, or could you have gotten the primary benefit from a two-night stay? Did every meal have to be in a sit-down restaurant, or would a picnic lunch with sandwiches from a deli or even Subway™ be a satisfactory, economical substitute? I am not asking you to lessen your enjoyment, just fine-tune it. Remember, we are focusing on the Extras category. We are looking for unnecessary or impulse spending first.

When you sit down with your spouse or family and discuss making changes to your spending habits, beware of only talking about cutting. Help them understand the long-term benefits of using that money elsewhere. That's how you get buy-in when it's time to cut back on grabbing fast food or downsizing expenses for a vacation. Be sure to include in the conversation what you plan to cut back so they don't think they're the only ones having to do this.

If you're like most people, when you look back at this exercise ninety days from now, you'll be pleasantly surprised at how little you missed those things. You'll be even more pleased with the money that became available for your wealth plan. You will use this money first to reduce your debt faster than you had planned before doing this work. If you've already eliminated your debt, you'll have this money to invest in your future wealth. Even if you only need to reduce your Extras category by $500 a month, that adds up to $6,000 a year. What kind of dent would that put in your debt? What good could come from having an additional $6,000 in an investment account today?

Next Level Work

At your ninety-day point, it's time to go to the next level. Average people would be happy to stay at this level, but I know you want more. I want more for you. So, I'm going to ask you to do the same exercise one more time. I need you to take another 25 percent off what's left in your Extras category. You can take another ninety days to do it. This time, it might be tougher. Or maybe it's easier because you've mentally decided to bet on your future self rather than consume everything today.

You may believe there's nothing left that you could live without and still enjoy your current lifestyle. Or you may have found it so easy to eliminate the first 25 percent that you look forward to the challenge of doing it again. The basis of this exercise is to find money that isn't serving you on your wealth path and put it to work for your future.

Doing the exercise might bring up some negative feelings. It may even bring a tear to your eye. You may feel that the loss of something familiar is more powerful than the gain of something better in the future. That's normal. Once you see your net worth begin to increase, those negative feelings will go away.

It seems all I'm doing is asking you to give up something, tighten your spending, have less fun, and sacrifice. If you want to look at it that way, you certainly can. However, most of my clients find that the Extras category is composed primarily of mindless spending. The feeling of "loss" only comes about because now they're seeing it. It didn't feel like a loss when that money slipped right through their fingers.

When you keep in mind that the achievement of your wealth plan is what's really important, instead of "giving up" something, you are looking for "found money." It becomes a treasure hunt, and the high you get from discovering where it's been hiding far outweighs any negative feelings you may experience.

CHAPTER 11

Time Blocking

WHILE DEVELOPING THE content for this program, I asked myself why so few people achieve wealth. I realized that most fail to dedicate specific blocks of time each week to evaluate where they are in their wealth journey. They don't even know where they are, much less what their next steps should be.

Most of us work forty to forty-five hours each week. When I ask my clients how many hours each week they spend money, for example, going to the grocery store, buying stuff on Amazon, shopping for clothes, etc., the typical answer is around five hours. My next question is this: How much time do you spend each week managing or taking care of your money? For most, the answer is thirty minutes. This means only 1 percent of the time dedicated to earning and spending money is spent managing it. One percent. Let that sink in.

When only 1 percent of your earning and spending time is put toward managing money, how good do you think the results will be? Compare this with other areas of your life. If you spend 1 percent of your time with your kids, would you call yourself a good parent? What would your relationship with a spouse or significant other be like if you only allotted 1 percent of your time to them?

There's a quote in the Bible I like for this. It's Matthew 6:21: "For where your treasure is, there your heart will be also." What this means is that our hearts follow what we value. When you relate this to time, how much value are you putting on your "treasure" if you only dedicate 1 percent of your "money use time" to managing it?

Since you have a wealth vision and are committed to working on your plan to achieve it, let's dedicate more time to it. I want you to increase the amount of time you manage your money by 400 percent. Don't let that number scare you. It comes out to two hours per week.

Just like finding money in your Extras category of spending, we are going to find time in your schedule. Increasing the amount of time spent managing your money will require you to change some habits. If you feel like you simply "don't have time," the reality is likely that you simply haven't MADE time. Prepare yourself to say "no" to something in your life that is not serving you in order to come up with the time to manage your money. Is there anything that immediately hits you that you can identify and change?

Some of the biggest wastes of time noted in the news include watching non-educational television programs, scrolling social media platforms, and playing video or other games by yourself. I'm not being hardcore here and suggesting you eliminate those things completely. I recognize there is value in having some downtime and following the news, friends, and family's posts online. I am asking you to create awareness about how much time you're spending on these things. Look at the daily average of your screen time on your phone. It might be a shock. Take advantage of the focus settings on your phone to carve out the time needed for money management because it's so vital to your current and future success.

I use a strategy called time blocking for everything that is important to me. Time blocking is a time management technique where you divide your day into dedicated blocks of time to complete the tasks you deem essential. It helps you to maximize your focus and increase productivity by minimizing distractions. I challenge you to block time not just to manage your money but to educate yourself about how money works and potential investments. Some of this education might even come from those much-loved social media platforms. Seek out financial experts and follow them to plug a little knowledge into your scrolling time.

Make Your Morning Routine Powerful

We all have habits for how we begin each day. We have our morning routines. The question is this: Have you chosen your routine or has it developed by default? Do you drag yourself out of bed, start the coffee, and jump in the shower? Or have you developed a more powerful routine to start your day, such as this:

- Get up at the same time every morning.
- Go to the gym, for a run, or exercise at home.

- Wind down from exercise with a brief meditation.
- Read something positive or helpful for the day ahead while having your coffee.
- Journal or note how what you read will impact your day.
- Read your affirmations as you start the shower.

One of the most beneficial books I have read about how to start your day is *The Miracle Morning* by Hal Elrod. It's a personal development book that aims to help readers improve their lives right from the moment they open their eyes each day. The author recommends six specific steps that impact all areas of life. I used his suggestions to create the foundation for my routine to serve my mental and physical needs, then added fifteen minutes dedicated to reviewing my financials.

My best advice is for you to begin blocking fifteen minutes each Monday through Thursday to analyze your finances. Block this time in your calendar. Treat it as if it's the most important meeting of the day, preferably in the morning before you start your workday.

Here's what I want you to take a look at:

1. Your bank account
    a. What is your balance?
    b. What expenses hit yesterday?
    c. What's going out today? Is there enough in the account to cover it?
    d. Is there anything you need to dispute? Anything that is a surprise expense or credit? Question every transaction whether it is still serving you or it is time to make changes.

2. Your credit cards
    a. What are the most recent charges? Again, consider whether each transaction is moving you toward or away from your path to wealth.
    b. What is your total balance due, and when does the next payment need to be made?
    c. What is your remaining amount available before hitting your credit limit?

The purpose of this quick review is to keep your financial information front and center in your awareness. Add anything you need to address to your "to-do" list, and get it done.

Do you remember my reference to puzzles? The time you spend reviewing your financials Monday through Thursday is similar to the step of turning over all the puzzle pieces so you can see what you're working with. Doing so consistently allows you to prioritize your actions and complete your wealth plan.

This small investment of time is not meant to make huge pivots in your life. It is intended to keep you aware and keep your focus on the real prize. The worst thing that can happen is that we stop paying attention. Failing to pay attention, review financials, and take note of our spending can end up costing us more money and time later. Being on the journey requires you to focus on moving forward more often than backward. And when something pulls you back—and it will—you will be able to reverse direction more quickly and move forward again.

In addition to your Monday-through-Thursday quick review, I recommend setting aside one full hour every Friday,

Saturday, or Sunday, depending on your schedule, to look at the bigger picture. I highly recommend doing this early in your morning. When you do this first thing, you won't allow other distractions of the day to keep you from doing it.

This is where you start to put your financial puzzle together. It's where you pull out your Wealth Tracker and plan how you'll bring everything into alignment. You'll plan your goals for the week and review the ones you need long term. You'll also increase your awareness of the type of assets that will add to your net worth. Think about these questions:

- What opportunities am I seeking?
- How do I need to grow or balance my assets?
- What is the status of my liabilities? When and how will I pay them?
- Is everything aligned to achieve my wealth plan?

You'll want to eliminate distractions during this time. The purpose of these longer sessions is to help you anticipate what's coming. It's when you take inventory of your current financial situation and where you're headed in the next week or so. During this session, you will be looking ahead and deciding what actions to take to be prepared for whatever is next. Review your wealth goals during this hour. Ask yourself these additional questions:

- Is there a problem I need to address?
- How well am I doing with my goals? Am I on or off track?
- Do I need to pivot from my current plan?
- What should I anticipate happening?

After reviewing your wealth goals, take a look at your debt. Are you on track to pay it off? Has anything changed since last week? Is there an increase in income that you can use against bad debt?

The next step is to take a look at your assets. Consider whether your assets are still serving you. Are they growing? Is there room to leverage any of your assets?

The end goal here is to make you more aware of where your money is going and create new habits that will be of greatest service to your wealth plan. If you've done okay by reviewing your finances for only thirty minutes each week, just imagine how much better you will do when you invest two hours per week. Believe me when I tell you these simple habits will serve you well on your journey toward wealth.

The first eleven chapters of this book have been geared toward your personal finances: your vision, your awareness, how you think about money and why, determining where you are today with your spending, debt, and net worth, and dedicating time to improve in all those areas. That makes you, of course, the Chief Financial Officer of your personal finances. In the next six chapters, we are going to focus on how to create a healthy system to manage finances for a business. Whether you own or partner in a small business as an entrepreneur or if your hobby is a relatively small side gig, you are the CFO of your business finances as well. It's vital that you learn how to be a good one.

PART THREE

CHAPTER 12

Chief Financial Officer (CFO)

EVEN WHEN YOUR business is large enough to have a Chief Financial Officer (CFO) on staff, the financial success of your business is ultimately in your hands. In this chapter, we will look at how you are doing as the CFO and how you might improve.

When coaching my business clients, one of the first questions I ask is: Is your business reflecting the lifestyle you desire to live and the legacy you want to leave? Some are quite surprised by that question because they view their business as mostly "about the money," not the lifestyle or legacy.

Most entrepreneurs launch their businesses because they've developed a product they believe will make them financially successful. Other entrepreneurs rely on start-ups to pursue a passion, be their own boss, or simply for the satisfaction of building something from the ground up. When I dig deeper with questions, they begin to understand what I'm getting at.

To be truly satisfying, your business needs to support both the lifestyle you want to have and the legacy you want to create. After studying hundreds of businesses, both successful and unsuccessful, and talking with independent contractors, entrepreneurs, and hobbyists, I have learned that truly successful businesses don't kill their creators with stress. They don't allow important personal relationships to take a back seat. They don't control their owners. The owners control the businesses. The businesses are designed to support the lifestyle and legacy the owners desire.

As the CFO of your business, I want you to become aware of how you view the money involved in your business. How do you plan for the financial future of your business? And, like we did with your personal financials, how do you keep it all organized? There are specific, important steps for CFOs to take to make wise decisions for their businesses.

Step 1 - Invest Time Thinking About the Business

In my experience, the quality of our work is determined by the quality of our thinking. Before I begin any work, I take a moment to focus and mentally prepare. I remind myself why I am doing this and what I hope to accomplish. I remove all distractions. I put my phone away and sit, beginning to process through a series of questions:

- What am I trying to achieve and why?
- What is my greatest opportunity?
- What is my most significant liability?

- What needs to be done today?
- What two things can I marry together to make life better and easier?
- What can I eliminate?

It's a brief period of realignment with my goals and the opportunity or task. When I do that, I know the work will be better than if I hadn't taken that moment.

As I began coaching struggling business owners, I sought the underlying reasons for their struggles. What I found was that while they concentrated on making more and more money, they weren't paying enough attention to where it was going or how to keep more of it.

They learned to think of their business as a bucket that needs to be filled. Plans were made to fill the bucket with sales in the hopes of needing a bigger bucket or multiple buckets in the not-too-distant future. The problem with most businesses' buckets is that they have holes in them. When we are not taught to notice these holes, money flows out, and our businesses suffer as a result. Sadly, I've seen people who have been in business for thirty years who have little or nothing to show for it at the end of their working days. It's not that they didn't work hard. They made a lot of money. They just didn't give enough thought to the condition of their bucket, never patching the holes that allowed money to flow out.

Some common holes to consider include the following:

- They didn't analyze monthly expenses.
- They spent a lot on luxury vehicles.
- They had higher-than-necessary marketing budgets.

- They kept paying for goods and services that were no longer needed.
- They didn't increase the number and quality of people in their circle.
- They either failed to pivot or failed to innovate.
- They paid employees a lot more than the value of the jobs they did.

Most of us, as CFOs, live reactionary financial lives. That means we make our decisions based on what recently happened instead of what we want to happen in the future. This is often described as constantly "putting out fires." We fear slowing down enough to just think about our businesses.

As the CFO, investing time in thinking about money is part of your job. Far too many people default to negative thinking about money. They say things like, "Well, Austin, I find it hard to plan for what's next when I don't have enough money today." Or "I don't know if I'm going to have enough." I tell them that with that mindset, it's highly unlikely they will have money in the future, especially if they are unwilling to change their thought patterns.

Read on for the areas I have found to be the most valuable for increased thought and attention.

1. Risk Management

I want you to invest time thinking about risk management. Do you lean more toward being conservative with the company money, or are you more aggressive when thinking about where and how to invest? If you are conservative, are there seasons in your industry in which it's better to be a little more aggressive to earn the highest return on effort or investment? And vice versa.

Another consideration within the area of risk management is where you are in the life of your company. Are you just getting started and in a building phase? Maybe your business has plateaued, and you are trying to decide what direction to go. Or are you closer to the end of your involvement, where you might be thinking about selling or even ending your business, or somewhere in between? Do you have access to a lot of capital or very little?

A lot of my clients are busy with the day-to-day grind, and that's understandable. My job is to get them to mentally step back and take in the larger picture. Here are the questions I ask:

- Are you on track or off track to achieve your goals for the year?
- If someone else were doing all the day-to-day work, how would you think about the rest of the business, and what might you decide differently?
- What is the next season for your business? What does that mean, financially, for the business, and how can you prepare for that today? Note that if you can't *do* anything about what's coming, you can at least mentally prepare for it.

Every decision you make has some kind of effect on your future business. It's never wise to make any financial decisions in haste. I've learned this: The right opportunity at the wrong time is the wrong opportunity. Say yes to wrong decisions too many times, and your business could take a year or more to recover. And time is not on your side. You can always find or earn more money, but not more time. So, taking recovery time into consideration for potential risky opportunities is important. One of the most important jobs of a CFO is to treat their time with the same respect they give to their money. They invest time thinking about and anticipating risk.

Like we covered in the personal section of this book, you will want to choose a path and weigh every decision against whether it takes you closer to or away from your ultimate vision for the business. Set aside a specific time each week to focus on your business.

There's a saying about making whatever subject you need to learn into your favorite hobby. When I began my wealth journey, I needed to learn everything. I mentioned that I sought out coaches, experts, and mentors—anyone who was farther ahead on their wealth journey—and I took in their advice. Now, full disclosure: along my journey, I found that most people who are great at one aspect of life, whether it's spiritual, personal, family, business, or financial, are typically good at only one or two of those areas. What that means is they were likely to lack growth or stability in the others. I share this to remind you that, just because someone you look up to is excelling financially, does not mean they are a great spouse or parent. Take advice in areas where they excel and leave the other subjects to those who excel in other areas.

At one point, I was at a conference where David Allen was the keynote speaker. David Allen's book *Getting Things Done* is about a productivity system that helps individuals manage their tasks, commitments, and ideas by capturing everything in an organized, external system. The method emphasizes clearing mental clutter to reduce stress and increase focus, allowing for efficient and effective action on what is most important. My big takeaway from his talk was that I needed to schedule thinking time. I even wrote it in my journal in large letters.

Later that evening, I was having dinner with a few other attendees and one of my coaches. As I looked around the restaurant, I saw David Allen sitting alone and decided to go speak with him. My coach advised against it because I had enjoyed a few adult beverages. I went against his advice, sat down next to David, and introduced myself.

As it turns out, Mr. Allen had also been enjoying an adult beverage. I remembered him mentioning this in his keynote that he enjoys wine. It was a subtle joke when he made it, but I caught it. I was now wondering if he had been joking or if what he said was real. I was about to find out.

When I thanked him for his presentation, his first and very direct question to me was, "What was the one thing you got out of today?"

I opened my journal and showed him in large letters with a huge star next to it, *THINKING TIME.*

He listened as I talked about it and said, "You're not (expletive) going to do it."

His tone was aggressive and passionate, and initially, it shocked me. But I immediately matched it and said, "Yes, I (expletive) am!"

He replied once again with, "No, you are (expletive) not!"

At this point, my coach, who was witness to the exchange, gave me the "do not engage" signal from across the room. I wasn't having it. And what resulted was a lively and beautiful conversation for the next ninety minutes that I'll never forget.

As it turned out, David was right. It took several years before I implemented his advice to add thinking time to my schedule. Even when something sounds like a great idea, and you believe you understand what it means, it can take years before you truly understand the entire concept and how it can fit into your life.

If you look at my schedule today, you will see that I have blocked a full hour several days each week as "thinking time." This is when I take a walk in the woods near my home. I ask myself all the important questions about life and my business:

- Am I using my gifts and talents as God intended?
- What area of my life needs my focus right now?
- What is my biggest opportunity?
- What is my biggest liability?
- What season of life am I currently in?
- What is the next season in my life that I should begin preparing for?
- What do I need to do with my financials to better align them to my vision?
- What do I need to eliminate?
- With all these thoughts, what do I need to focus on in the next seven to thirty days?

And with my coaching business, I ask:

- What do I need to do?
- What do I need to stop doing?

- How do I make my assets work better for me?
- What should I buy or sell?
- Who should I talk to?
- Who should I stop talking to?

As you can imagine, those questions fill up those hours pretty quickly. And I thank David Allen, every time, for challenging me with the truth about implementing his valuable advice. Allowing yourself time to think is the most valuable use of your time as the CFO. You can't solve future problems or take advantage of future opportunities if you are not thinking about the future. Your future will happen whether you think about it or not. I can tell you, from experience, that your future will be better when you slow down and invest time in thinking about what you have and how that can align with what you want.

2. *Plan for the Future*

The next important concept for the CFO to consider is planning for the future. I've mentioned that I am a perpetual student. I may not be smart in a lot of ways, but I am smart enough to put myself in rooms with people who are smarter than I am and listen to what they have to say. One of the people I have been blessed to learn from is Tony Robbins, a world-renowned motivational speaker, best-selling author, and life strategist who has coached millions on achieving personal and financial success. The number one thing he taught me was to anticipate the future, to consider possibilities, to envision things that have not yet occurred, and even events that might never take place.

Anticipating the future is a great exercise. It makes you stretch your brain and strengthen your thinking muscles. It helps you notice the little things that can make a big difference in the outcome. There's a great book called *The Noticer* by Andy Andrews. It is an educational instruction manual for life. It teaches you to anticipate the needs around you, whether they involve supporting others, improving your business, or recognizing new opportunities that could help it grow. I highly recommend it to help you better plan for the future.

Right now, are you able to anticipate what might happen in your business in the next three to six months? Can you guess, with some accuracy, where your financials might be at that time? Of course, there's always a chance life will throw a curveball, and your guess could be off by a mile. What's important here is always to be thinking three to six months out so you make better decisions today.

When you look forward, you often gain a clearer understanding of your true opportunities. As a leader of a business, lots of opportunities are bound to come your way. They all require time to evaluate. Evaluating them may require financial or legal commitments. When you allow yourself time to think (step 1) *and* plan for the future (step 2), you'll be better prepared to weigh the value of those opportunities and determine which are truly beneficial to your business. When you sift through the details of what appear to be opportunities, you may discover they are nothing more than distractions.

3. *Keep Your Financials Organized*

It's incredible how quickly things can get disorganized as your business grows and opportunities require your attention. That's why successful CFOs build a team of experienced professionals around them. In the beginning, unfortunately, you may be a team of one. But, in time, the goal is to have others take on the grind so you can focus on that larger picture. Before you are able to hire these professionals, rely on outside sources that offer the necessary services to multiple clients. So, who do you need?

First, you will want to have a Certified Public Accountant (CPA). At the very least, have a CPA do the taxes for your business. Any competent CPA will help you become better organized as they collect the necessary information. They'll also educate you as to what you can and cannot deduct. If you don't have training in accounting, you probably aren't even aware of how many deductions are possible for businesses. A good CPA will show you ways to recover at least their fee for doing your taxes, likely more.

Early in my career, I handled my own taxes because there wasn't much to my business. I figured it wasn't necessary to go to a CPA for that service. I later learned that it was actually costing me *not* to rely on a professional.

The second person you want on your team is a competent bookkeeper. Again, in the beginning, I was the bookkeeper, but not a "competent" one. Could I learn to use software such as QuickBooks? Sure. Did I want to? No. I wanted to stay focused on my strengths, which were creating new ways to grow my business. Every hour I spent on bookkeeping was an hour I wasn't generating income. Yes, certain responsibilities come with being the CFO of your business, but it's always important to play to your strengths and pay others to handle your weaknesses.

The third type of person to have on your team may not be just one person. Fulfilling this need may require several people. What I'm talking about here is your coaches or mentors. Throughout history, there has been an overwhelming amount of advice about seeking wisdom from others, from the Bible to John Maxwell.

> Proverbs 1:5 says, "A wise man will hear, and will increase learning; and a man of understanding shall attain unto wise counsels."

> Proverbs 11:14 says, "Where there is no guidance, a people falls, but in an abundance of counselors there is safety."

> And from John C. Maxwell: "The people closest to me determine my level of success or failure. The better they are, the better I am. And if I want to go to the highest level, I can do it only with the help of other people."

As the CFO, it's important to have people who can help you understand the money your business generates, and the spending required to grow it even more. Your mentors could be in your life for years. Some may be in your life for a season. With others, you may learn only from their stories and experiences, possibly from reading a book or listening to a podcast, for example. Maybe you even learn from relative strangers just by asking them questions about their lives. Remember Brandon, the taxi driver?

I discovered some financial mentors within my own client database while selling real estate. They may not have been outwardly wealthy, but as we got deeper into their transactions, I learned they had millions. I would always ask what they did to achieve their success and what lessons they learned along the way to wealth. Early on, I found something extremely helpful: most of these clients had owned rental real estate at some point. However, few still owned the properties when we spoke. Most sold because they tried to manage the rentals themselves and found it was more work than it was worth.

From those conversations, I deduced that if I were to develop my own real estate portfolio of rentals, managing it myself would create an unwanted liability. If I decided to own rentals, I would need to hire out the property management aspect, which I did. I compare this to my clients who are doctors. They signed up to be doctors for the financial aspects of that career, not to be janitors in their own offices. My rentals are an investment of my money, not my time, and that decision has made all the difference in both my quality of life and my net worth.

Organizing Like a CFO

From the beginning of your business all the way to the end, whether you sell it or give it as an inheritance, it's vital to have all of your financial information organized in one place and the right people in place to help you do so. This is the same principle we covered when talking about your personal finances. You may have to fight to simplify your financial information. However, simplifying is the best way to stay on top of your current progress and plan for the future.

Here's an example. In the beginning, you may have a single bank account. As you grow, there may be a need for multiple accounts or to work with more than one bank because a different type of bank serves a specific need for your business. Every time your needs change, you will need to revisit your system's organization to ensure there's one place where you can look at everything at a glance.

Let's consider your business taxes. First, are they being done? Are you current with what your business owes the government? Hopefully, the CPA you put on your team will ensure this happens. Where are the filed taxes? Are they stored electronically or in paper form? Are they all together? If asked, can you easily look back at four, five, or even seven years of past tax filings? For corporate income taxes, at the time of this writing, it's advised to keep records for four years from the due date or when the return is filed, whichever is later. You need to keep records for seven years if you file a claim for a loss from worthless securities or bad debt deductions. So, I use seven years as my standard for all business documentation.

The next area you want to keep organized is all your financial apps. As you grow, as your business grows, and as your thinking develops, so will the tools that you utilize. You'll want access to all of them in one place and to ensure they are all kept up to date.

Here's a quick example of how I do it: If you were to open my phone, you'd see a single file containing all of the apps I use to track my financials. Keeping them all together saves time. I can review the financial aspects of my life and business within seconds and quickly make informed decisions about any necessary moves.

How do you feel now about being the virtual CFO of your business? The realization of the commitment and responsibilities involved in owning a business can be unsettling. Knowing that the "buck" not only stops with you but that it's your job to manage every buck that flows through your business properly is vital to its success. Taking advantage of the systems and advice in this book should give you an advantage.

CHAPTER 13

The Wealth Machine

PERSONALLY, I BELIEVE this building block in the Cheviron Pyramid of Wealth is the most significant for making strides in your wealth journey. Everything we have covered to this point has been preparation. Here, I will show you the exact system I used to get my wealth journey on the right path. It helped me completely transform my attitude toward my money and my ability to use it to my best advantage.

I've met many people who struggled to achieve wealth. It wasn't that they were unintelligent. It wasn't that they did not earn enough or gave their management insufficient thought. Their problem was that they simply didn't have a system to properly manage the money they were earning. That was my problem, too.

At my lowest point, with a toddler and newborn, being on welfare, I knew something had to change. I had to change the way I viewed my life, my responsibilities as a husband and parent, and how I managed my finances. I understood that if I ran the same play over and over, I'd get the same results. It's the same lesson you learn with video games. There are always patterns in the game. Once you know them, you can win more often and faster.

So, I went in search of a system to fix all my money problems, and guess what? I didn't find one. None of the people in my world were having the success I wanted with their money. To be clear, I wasn't looking at how much money they were making but how much they kept and put to work for them.

I came to the realization that I was going to have to create my own system that would allow me to move more effectively and efficiently toward my life's vision. What follows is what I call the Wealth Machine. It's one of the most powerful building blocks in the Cheviron Pyramid of Wealth. It has made all the difference in my wealth journey, and I encourage you to take advantage of it for you.

The System

When creating a system, you usually focus on fixing a single aspect of your broader challenge, then you observe, determining how well it's working. From there, you look for ways to improve it. What I initially discovered was that one of the biggest problems holding me back was that all the money I was earning was being deposited into a single account. It was going into the same account from which I was spending money. That made it too easy to spend it all. The more money

I had in the account, the richer I felt and the more I spent. Then, when I spent it all, I felt broke and made decisions with a scarcity mindset. And there's no way to make the right decisions when you're in the wrong emotional state. That point, I believe, is the foundation of a lot of the money problems in the world.

How do we avoid that? We rethink where we put our money. First, we must change how we think about our primary bank account. Notice I said "primary." That means "main," as in the most important of more than one. Before jumping in to use this system, you will have to research the policies around having more than one account with your bank. Some banks have policies around how many accounts you can have. There may be fees involved for each, and so on. Once you start using the Wealth Machine, you may find that your current bank is no longer the right one for you. That's a decision you will make after understanding how the Wealth Machine works.

Let's get back to your primary account. Up to this point, you probably called it your "checking account." I want you to start thinking of it as your "Deposit Account." Its only purpose, going forward, is to be a landing place for all the income you generate. It's a "holding" account, not a "spending" account. Once your money is there, you use the rest of the system to control how it is managed. If this were your only account, you would be 100 percent more tempted to spend it without much thought to saving for important things like taxes and your future. I refer to this Deposit Account as the hub or center of the Wealth Machine.

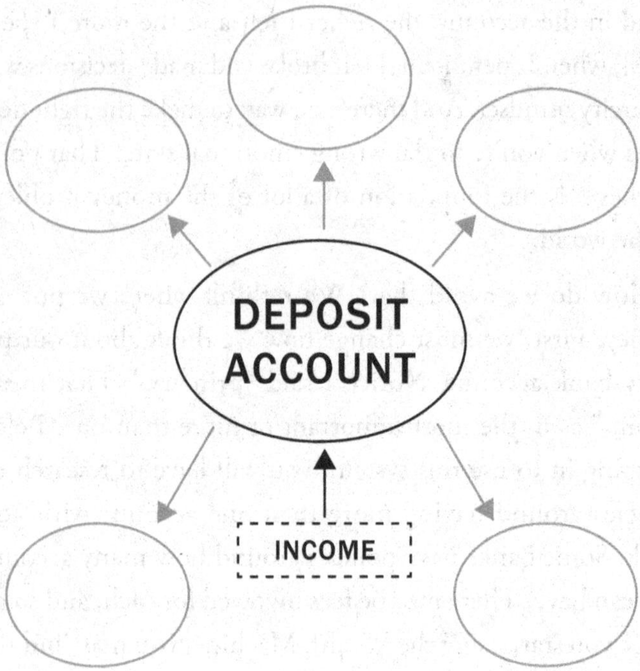

The next account to set up is the "Tax" account. This is a separate savings account. This is absolutely necessary if you own a business, are self-employed, or an independent contractor. In 2023, nearly one in four Americans indicated they were behind in paying their taxes. That's millions of people who are carrying the weight of debt to the government. And that, my friend, is not a good feeling.

Why are there so many unpaid taxes? There are numerous excuses, most of which boil down to poor money management. But that's not going to be you because you are setting up a specific account to hold the money you will owe the government at tax time. When asking a CPA whether there's an advantage to waiting to pay taxes closer to tax time versus on the dates estimated taxes are due, the answer I received was "send it in as soon as you receive the money." Hopefully, you receive money more often than quarterly, when the government suggests payments be made. Rather than sending a bunch of checks to the US Treasury, I want you to move your tax money from the deposit account to a separate tax account as soon as you receive it.

How much do you set aside? The government wants a percentage of what you generate. Your goal is not to send so much that the government owes you a refund, but also not to send too little, so you owe a significant amount at tax time, with interest. This is where we rely on the experts we have on our team. Ask the person who does your taxes to give you the average tax percentage versus the income you have paid in the last few years. It might be 30 percent; it might be 20 percent.

In my case, we determined that 20 percent is a solid number. So, during my fifteen-minute review of my financial situation every Monday through Thursday morning, I do the math for any new money in my deposit account. I immediately transfer 20 percent of any new deposits to my tax account. It sits there until it's time to send in my estimated taxes. This quick and easy transfer of funds that weren't mine to spend anyway eliminates my excuses for not staying up to date with my taxes. When tax time rolls around in April, if my numbers were off in either direction, paying too much or too little, I adjust my percentage for subsequent transfers from my deposit account. What do you think happens if I owe less than I've set aside in the Tax account? I get to keep it! I either add it to my business account, if there's a need, or transfer it to my personal account.

My ultimate goal, with taxes, is to either owe a dollar or receive a dollar in return. That's how close I strive to be with the money I owe the government. I don't want them to have extra that I could be using to invest or spend. And I don't want to owe them more than I have placed in my tax account. If I do owe more, I will get with my CPA to work out a revised percentage to transfer to that tax account for the next tax cycle.

Do you know how empowered it makes me feel when my CPA says it's time to pay estimated taxes, and I simply ask, "How much?" and confidently write out the check because I have the money readily available? It's amazing, and I want you to experience that feeling, too. Open the tax account and start the habit of moving that money.

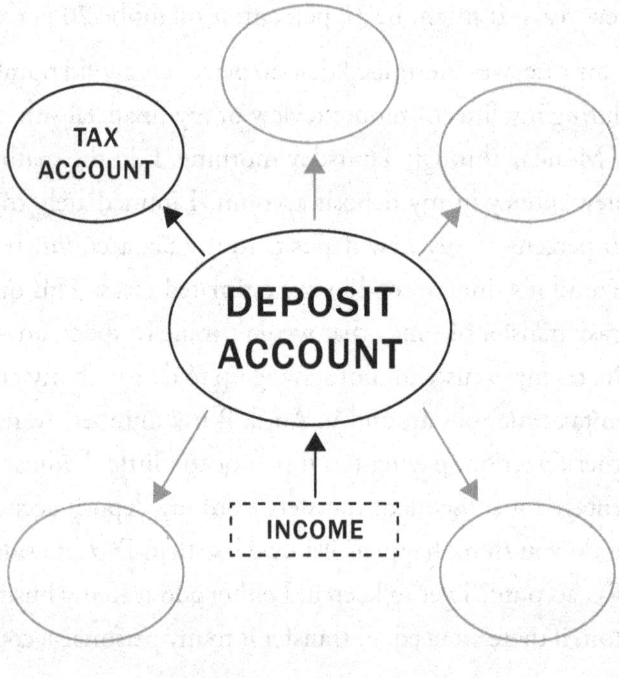

The next account to open will be dedicated to helping build your financial wealth. We will refer to this account as "Invest." You are going to make a dedicated commitment to putting money into this account to work for you. When a viable opportunity comes your way that requires a financial investment, you will be able to take advantage of it because of this account. This is another area where you'll use a percentage to determine how much to move into this account.

If you've never read it, I highly recommend the book *The Richest Man in Babylon* by George Samuel Clason. In the book, it says, "No less than ten percent of what you earn should be yours to keep." At the time I read that, I wasn't keeping any of my money. I was spending it all on things like

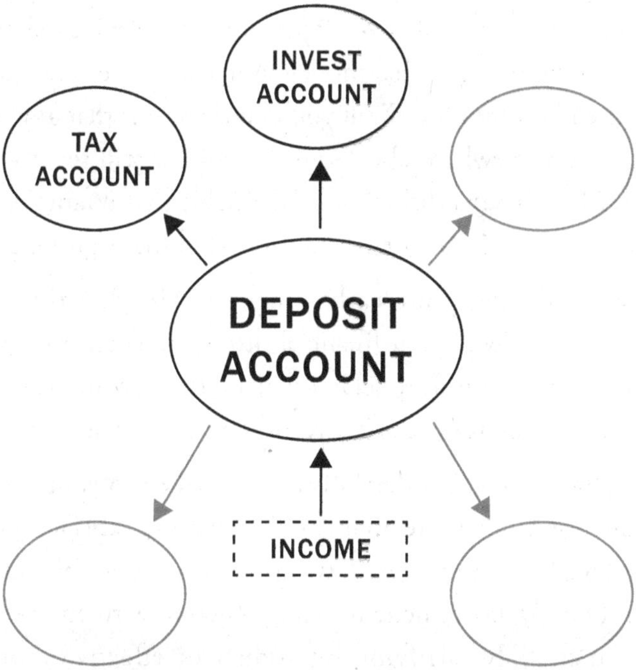

my mortgage, clothes, and other bills, bills, and more bills. I didn't feel that I was in control of my finances, and I certainly didn't set aside any money to grow my wealth. I want you to determine the percentage that you will dedicate to investing. It can be no less than 10 percent, but it could be more—a lot more, especially when you get your spending on Extras down like we covered in Chapter 10.

If this is the first time you've even thought about setting aside money for growth, I would suggest starting with 10 percent. Now, I understand you might be thinking, "Austin, I don't have an extra 10 percent to invest in my future." I have personally heard that answer hundreds of times, and the most important time was when I said it to myself. I am happy to tell you that each time I was told that, the person was wrong. It is not that there is not an *extra* 10 percent available; it's that you are choosing to spend that money somewhere else. The question then becomes this: Will you choose to put that amount of money somewhere else? Somewhere that will serve your future? It's the establishment of the habit that counts more than the actual dollars being transferred in the beginning.

Again, during your early morning Monday through Thursday review of your financial situation, when you reach the Deposit Account, quickly calculate the new money that has come in and transfer 10 percent to your "Invest" account.

The next account to open is not dedicated to your financial situation. It's more about fulfillment and satisfaction in your life. Label this one "Giving." If you're not already a giver, I highly recommend it. Being generous with our wealth is an incredibly satisfying byproduct of effective money management. When we can give to support others, it's hard to feel poor. It's hard to feel anxious about money.

I recommend starting with a minimum of 1 percent. You will barely feel its absence, and you will be able to do great things with it. It will make you become a better person.

If you are already giving some of your money to other people or causes, I recommend working your way up in increments to moving 10 percent of every dollar you earn into this account. Again, you will do this during the regularly scheduled time each week that you review your financial situation. Build that habit!

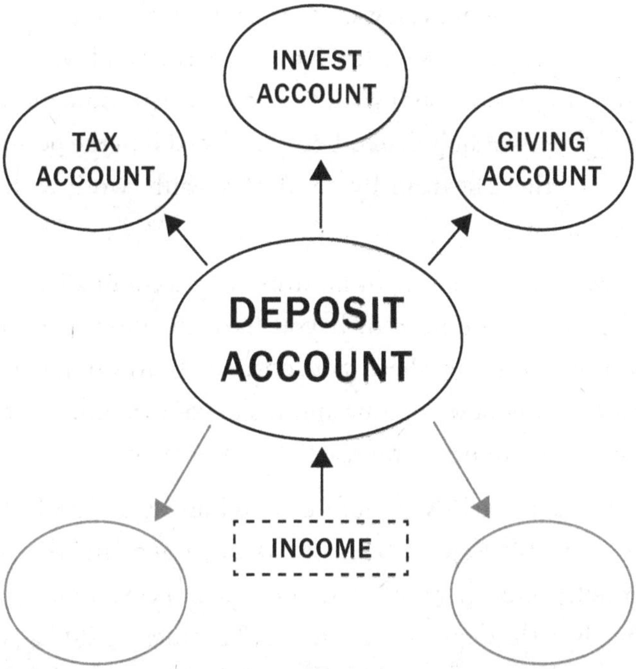

At this point, you may be wondering how much of your money you get to spend. When you take care of what's most important first and spend the rest, you live a more fulfilled life. We will move into the spending accounts next.

The next account you want to feed from your deposit account is your "Business Operations" account. This one is a checking account. You could possibly use a business checking account you already have for this. You just no longer put *deposits* in it. Money only comes into this account through *transfers* from your Deposit Account.

The goal here is to come up with a figure that will cover the expenses in your business until another transfer occurs. We are no longer using percentages like we did with the other accounts. The figure you want to use is whatever your budget is for your business expenses. Now, just as we did with your personal expenses, you'll want to consider that some months have higher spending than others. Like we did in the personal section of the Cheviron Pyramid of Wealth, work with an average amount.

Be aware that you might not fund this account all at once on the first of the month. If you have the money in your deposit account, go ahead and do that. If you don't, look forward to any new deposits and make your transfers as that money comes in until you reach your budget goal.

For example, let's say your business budget is $5,000. You might transfer $2,000 from the deposit account the first week of the month, another $2,000 when the next incoming money hits the deposit account, and another $1,000 a couple of weeks into the month. What's important is that you have the right amount of money in the business operations account when your business bills come due. Again, this is easy to manage when looking at your financial accounts five days a week.

I'll tell you right now that very rarely did I have all the money for my business expenses in my business operations account on the first few days of the month. But I *was* able to manage the flow from my deposit account into the business operations account as that money came in.

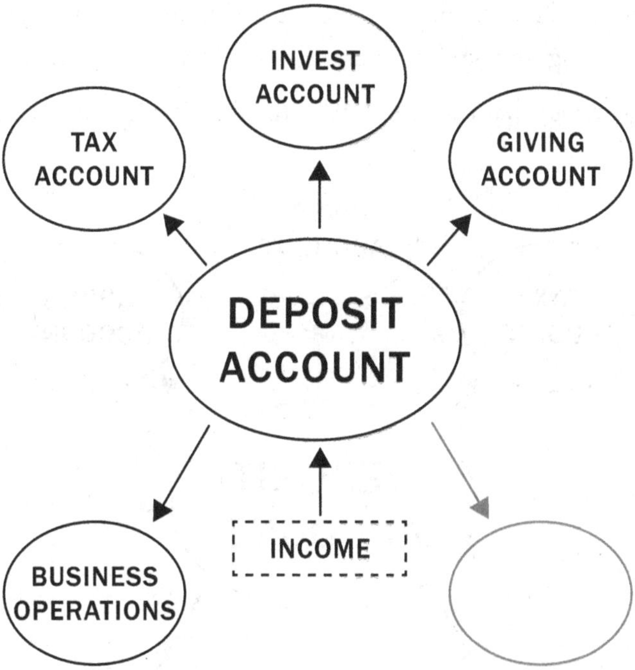

This last account is the one you have probably been waiting for. It's your "Personal Operations" account or your personal checking account.

This is the account you will fund with the amount we determined in Chapter 4 as your monthly average spending. What happens when you don't have enough in the deposit account to fund all of these? You have to decide whether you want all the lifestyle Extras, or if you want to move farther down the path toward the vision of your life from Chapter 2. Do you want your future? Or do you want what you have today? You either need to make some changes in your spending habits, or improve your skill at generating the money that goes into your deposit account. Unless you know of a change coming for your business where the deposits are increasing dramatically, you'll be focusing on your habits around business expenses first.

Below is what the whole Wealth Machine looks like:

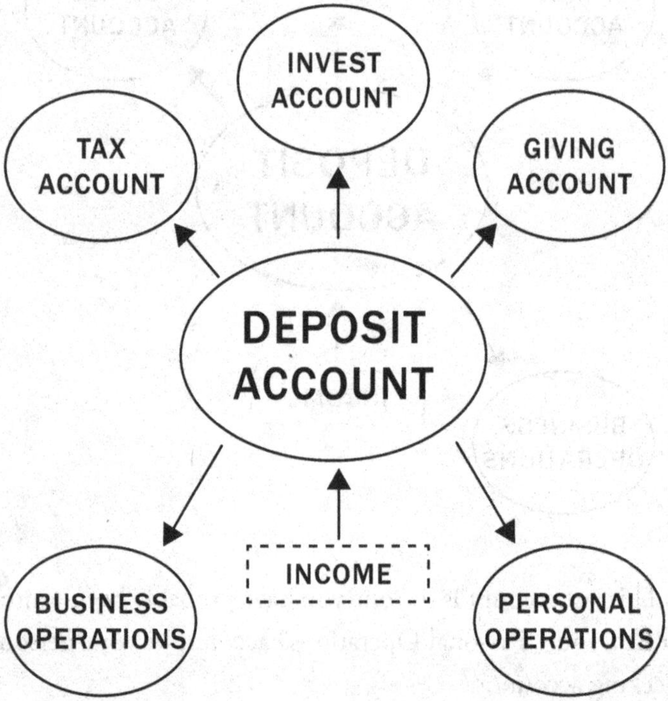

The first year of using the Wealth Machine is the most important because being consistent with transferring money into those other accounts will build a habit that will make a huge positive impact on your progress toward your vision. Each following year, evaluate whether you want to change some of the percentages. After the first year, I increased my investment account percentage. My investments were working for me, turning those dollars into more dollars. So, naturally, I wanted to do more of that. So, in the second year, I set aside 15 percent in my investment account. In the third year, I increased it to 20 percent. In the fourth year, I raised it to 25 percent, and in the fifth year, I added 33 percent of my deposit funds to my Invest Account.

Watching the dollars increase was almost an addiction for me because I knew they could make even more dollars for me. This motivated me to keep tightening my spending and increasing my income. I knew the more those dollars worked for me, the less I'd have to work to earn money in the future. My focus on money shifted from "What can I get today?" to "How can we live on less today to fund our future later?"

You may think 33 percent is too much to set aside to invest. That depends on how quickly you want to achieve your vision of wealth and your other financial responsibilities. In my case, by that fifth year, setting aside 33 percent of my deposit funds, I realized I was ahead of schedule for achieving wealth. My pace was faster than I needed it to be. I was ecstatic. My wife was happy, too, but had other thoughts about our pace. She asked me this: "Austin, if you died with all of this money, what does it matter? What if we slow down the pace and live a little more (a.k.a. spend) today to enjoy some more experiences, to create fun memories?"

You see, she is my opposite. I am almost always focused on being happy in the future. She is more focused on being happy in the present. So, what did we decide? I reduced the percentage for my Invest Account to 20 percent. At that rate, I would still hit my target for wealth in the time frame I had in mind. I continued to fund my vision, and our family started living a life we love.

This is the exact playbook I used to transform my financial life, going from welfare to achieving the wealth I had envisioned. Now, your investment number will likely be different from mine. That's okay. It's your vision of wealth that you are working toward. Using this tool, which has proven to work for me and many of my clients, will get you headed in the right direction.

CHAPTER 14

Cash Flow Management

BEFORE WE DELVE into this topic, I want you to understand your habits and emotions regarding having a substantial amount of money in your Deposit Account. What have your habits been in the past around receiving large deposits? Did you think, "Yay, I can take care of business and plan for growth," or was it more like "Yay, I can get that new car I've been looking at"? Receiving a large sum is an amazing feeling. It's rewarding. It's freeing. You may not have realized you were under some financial stress before it arrived, but then that feeling of relief came over you. If you remember from Chapter 3, your awareness of your feelings about money is critical to your success in managing it.

Even as a kid, when I got a relatively large sum of money, all I could think about was how I could make it earn even more. I was totally focused on the future, on investing. For my wife, receiving a large sum meant she could treat herself to something special, something out of the ordinary. We are fortunate to have realized that, together, we can achieve a healthy balance with our money, investing some for the future while having fun today.

On the other end of the money spectrum, how do you feel and act when there's not enough to cover your obligations? Have you burned out relationships by frequently asking for "a little help"? Are you living in a depressed state? Does having a negative cash flow month trigger something in you, maybe a lack of self-esteem? Does it make you angry and hard to be around? This awareness is important because you can use these insights to motivate you to stay on track by using the Wealth Machine. Before you can commit to a new plan, you have to understand what is and is not working with the old plan and accept the need and desire to change.

When you make the decision to build wealth, you're going to realize there are a million other decisions to make along the way. You will start to question nearly every dime you spend. "Is this something we really want or need, or can the amount of this purchase contribute to our future wealth instead?" It can be tough at first to see how a relatively small amount can make a difference. It's much easier to go ahead and spend small amounts now and only seek out larger amounts for your big, future plans. It's always your choice to do that.

When I took a closer look at my smaller spending habits, I learned that their accumulated value added up to some pretty large figures. And, in most cases, while working on my wealth plan, I decided to forgo those small purchases and invest the money instead. Doing so was like pouring gasoline on a fire.

Everything in my wealth plan accelerated, and in the end, we didn't mind the pinch of skipping those smaller spends.

Some might think of this as "penny pinching." My wife and kids may have called me a "tightwad" behind my back during our lean months. I prefer to call it "cash flow management." That term elevated the value of what I was doing in my mind and changed my attitude completely around doing what it takes to achieve wealth.

At first, you might feel like you're broke as you decide to live on less. I did. My whole family did. We lived like we were broke for nearly ten years. Want to know what the good news was? We weren't. We were just focused on our building phase. And now that we have achieved the goal of wealth, we can live however we want. It may not take you ten years to achieve wealth. Remember, my starting point was being on welfare. You may already have a head start on your wealth journey because you are already managing your finances effectively. You may already have some investments or a positive net worth. You may already have some positive financial habits in place. If so, good for you! Let's take the next steps in managing your cash flow.

Seasons of Cash Flow

There are multiple seasons of cash flow. When you begin focusing on your wealth plan, you're going to make decisions about living on less. There may also be times when living on less hurts—a lot. I'll warn you that the first season is the toughest. As you start moving your money into the different accounts in the Wealth Machine that we covered in the previous chapter, you will likely stretch yourself thin. It will probably be uncomfortable at first, and that's okay. That's the season that you're in. Know that the seasons change, though.

In this season, to meet the needs of each account, you may have to borrow from other sources. Just like when you're broke, you will have to be creative about where you get money. I'll show you where it might come from in Chapter 18 when we go over the Money Wheel. In this chapter, we will focus on how you handle your incoming money, and how you can take proper care of it.

Your definition of seasons may vary from mine due to how you earn income. As I mentioned, I was a real estate agent. The natural ebb and flow of the business is that January and February tend to be slow in Northern Indiana. Spring and summer months are when the most real estate transactions occur, and sometimes in the fall. I would plan for the lean months either by setting aside extra earnings before the slow season began or by temporarily borrowing money to cover my costs until business picked up during the busier months.

Some businesses may have fewer slow months but instead have "seasons" that require higher expenses. For example, businesses that cater to vacationers, such as ski resorts or those in beach towns, often need extra help, and temporary staff are hired over the summer. More money is made during those times, but more is also spent. When you pay attention to your seasons, you'll be able to flatten out that financial roller coaster you might be on. You'll know when it's the right time to invest and when it's best to hold some cash in reserve.

What I did, using the Wealth Machine, was bury my money where I didn't allow ready access to it, but I could find it later when it was time to use it. It is like being a squirrel, right? They hide the nuts they find all summer in places they have access to in the winter.

If you've ever watched National Lampoon's *Vegas Vacation*, you'll remember that Clark Griswold got a little too much into gambling. He ran out of money but didn't want to tell his family. He asked Uncle Eddie for help. Eddie was happy to help, but there was one problem. Eddie had literally buried the money and forgotten where it was. Clark and Eddie headed out into the desert and started digging. What they found was a collection of coffee cans buried around the property, containing twenties, tens, and fives. When they added it all up, it was enough to help Clark pay off his gambling debt.

Your multiple accounts will seem small at first, maybe even so small that you doubt how effective they will be in your Wealth Machine. I can assure you that those small amounts will add up quickly and contribute significantly to your wealth achievement. It's the discipline of managing your money that will lead to wealth.

Outgoing Money

Our outgoing money falls into two categories: Fixed Expenses and Variable Expenses. It's essential that we understand the difference and consider which category every "spend" falls. When we don't pay attention to these categories and their expenses, we are likely to pay more than we need to today.

That means there will be less money available to invest in our future.

Fixed expenses are things we have signed up for. We have deemed them necessary for our business, and they are most often the same amount every month. They are predictable. This would include expenses such as rent for office space, utilities, and loans for equipment or vehicles necessary to keep our businesses running. We have previously agreed to these. Fixed expenses can cause huge problems with cash flow because many of us have higher fixed expenses than we actually need for our businesses. This happens simply because we stop paying attention. We pay the bills without questioning whether we need all of those expenses.

The other types of expenses are variable. These are the most dangerous ones. They may come out of the blue. An unexpected need may result in a $1,000 bill (or more). Think about a car repair, a medical bill, or even a last-minute trip you feel obligated to take. That's why it's so important to keep our variable expenses in check. Saying "yes" to a large variable expense in the wrong season could be financially devastating.

If you ever hang out with me and discuss money, you'll know that my mind is always on reducing my expenses without negatively impacting my business. This is especially true when I'm in a building season. During building seasons, I invest more of my time in product development and spend more money than usual on production. This means that I'm not taking as many actions to bring money into my business. I can do that because I have financially prepared for it.

There's so much waste in most of my clients' businesses. There is money going out that could be working for their wealth plan instead. To find it takes work. It takes commitment to stay on top of expenses and question every dollar spent. Most of us aren't doing that because we are focused on increasing our income. That's how most entrepreneurs are wired.

We are constantly evaluating how we can get a higher return on our investment in our businesses, on the time we put into product development, marketing, and customer service. The thought process is this: What do we need to do to bring in more sales and more money? Unfortunately, most often the answer is that we need to spend more to make more. And where does that additional money come from? Does it come from taking on new debt? Does it involve improving our skill level or the skills of our employees? Does it involve using new and better software? We all know that when we implement new software to improve things, the inevitable learning curve makes it feel like we are taking a couple of steps backward. For most of my clients, it adds a certain level of stress. There's a general acceptance that this is how it is if you want to get ahead in business.

I've taken the opposite approach. When I want or need more money for the growth of my business, the first place I look is at my variable spending. I ask myself, "What can I cut out of my expenses right now to help me fund the next step I have in mind for my business?" Do this for yourself right now. Ask yourself that same question. Reflect on the first answer that popped into your head. If it's truly feasible, something that won't cause harm to the function of your business, write it down. Then, do it or delegate it to someone in your company with a deadline for when it should happen. It can be that easy. If nothing came to mind when you asked yourself that question, you haven't been paying enough attention to your outgoing money. It's time to change that.

Demonstration of the Wealth Machine

Here's an example to provide extra motivation to get on top of your spending and demonstrate the power of the Wealth Machine in your business. We will transfer percentages from the Deposit Account to the Tax, Invest, and Giving Accounts. For the Business Account, let's assume we need $5,000 for the month, and we need $10,000 for the Personal Account.

Month One

First deposit = $6,000

- 20 percent ($1,200) gets transferred into the Tax Account.
- 10 percent ($600) transfers into the Invest Account.
- 1 percent ($60) goes into the Giving Account.
  This leaves us with $4,140 still in the Deposit Account. I'm going to split this between the Business and Personal Accounts, leaving a little in the Deposit Account. So, $2,000 transfers to each of those accounts, leaving $140 in the Deposit Account for now.

Second deposit = $8,000

- 20 percent ($1,600) gets transferred into the Tax Account.
- 10 percent ($800) transfers into the Invest Account.

- 1 percent ($80) goes into the Giving Account.

  This leaves us with $5,660 in the Deposit Account from this check. I'm going to split this between the Business and Personal Accounts, leaving a little in the Deposit Account. The split isn't even, and that's intentional. Each account serves a different purpose and has a different target. For example, the Personal Account is working toward a $10,000 funding goal, which requires more frequent and higher contributions than the Business Account. Personal expenses also tend to hit earlier in the month, so it helps to front-load that account. And truthfully, while we're aiming to create a repeatable system here, there's still an element of art to this process. No single formula will work perfectly every time, so we adapt our approach based on the specific situation. After transferring the funds to the Business and Personal Accounts, the Deposit Account now has only $660 remaining from this deposit.

Third deposit = $10,000

- 20 percent ($2,000) gets transferred into the Tax Account.
- 10 percent ($1,000) transfers into the Invest Account.
- 1 percent ($100) goes into the Giving Account.

  This leaves us with $7,560 in the Deposit Account. At this point, the Business Account only needs an additional $1,000 to achieve the budget, so that's all we will move from this check to that account. The Personal Account only needs another $5,000, so we'll move that as well. By managing the money from my Deposit Account, I now have the following:

- Tax Account = $4,800
- Invest Account = $2,400
- Giving Account = $240
- Business Account = $5,000
- Personal Account = $10,000
- Deposit Account = $1,560

What happens to that leftover money in the Deposit Account? It stays there. It's ready and waiting to feed the other accounts for next month.

Month Two might remain the same. We have the same dollar amount being deposited, and we will transfer the money exactly the same.

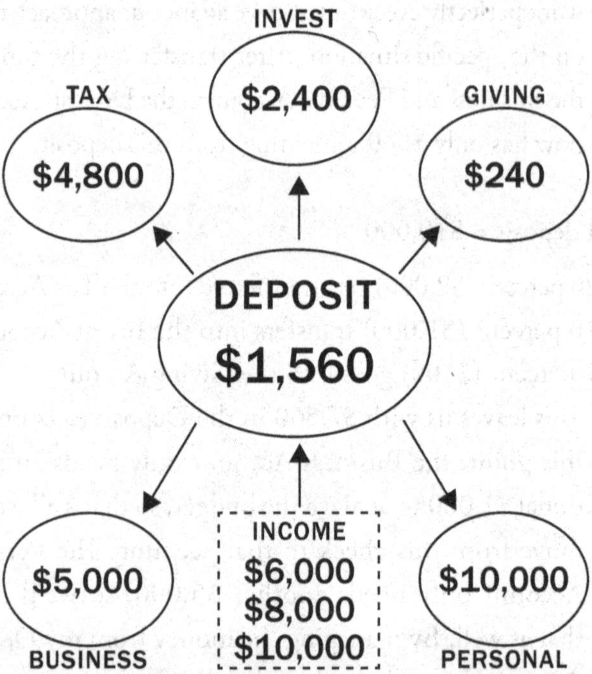

Month Two

First deposit = $6,000

- 20 percent ($1,200) gets transferred into the Tax Account.
- 10 percent ($600) transfers into the Invest Account.
- 1 percent ($60) goes into the Giving Account.

  This leaves us with $5,700 still in the Deposit Account (Because we added $6000 to the previous month's balance of $1,560, but subtracted the $1,200, $600, and $60 transfers with the new deposit for the new month, the new balance in the Deposit Account is now $5,700.) I'm going to split the $5,700 between the Business and Personal Accounts, transferring $2,000 to each of those accounts, leaving $1,700 in the Deposit Account as a buffer.

Second deposit = $8,000

- 20 percent ($1,600) gets transferred into the Tax Account.
- 10 percent ($800) transfers into the Invest Account.
- 1 percent ($80) goes into the Giving Account.

  With this second deposit in the second month, I added $1,700 to the new $8,000 deposit in the Deposit Account, bringing the balance to $9,700. When I transfer for the Tax, Invest, and Giving Accounts, this leaves us with $7,220 in the Deposit Account. I'm going to split this between the Business and Personal accounts, leaving a little in the Deposit Account. So, $2,000 transfers to the Business Account and $3,000 into the Personal Account, leaving a total of $2,220 in the Deposit Account.

Third deposit = $10,000

- 20 percent ($2,000) gets transferred into the Tax Account.
- 10 percent ($1,000) transfers into the Invest Account.
- 1 percent ($100) goes into the Giving Account.

When we add the third deposit of $10,000 and subtract the Tax, Invest, and Giving amounts, this leaves us with $9,120 in the Deposit Account. At this point, the Business Account only needs an additional $1,000 to reach its budget, so that's all we will transfer from this check to that account. The Personal Account only needs an additional $5,000 to be fully funded, so we will proceed with that as well. By managing the money from my Deposit Account, I now have the following:

- Tax Account = $9,600
- Invest Account = $4,800
- Giving Account = $480
- Business Account = $5,000
- Personal Account = $10,000
- Deposit Account = $3,120

The remaining amount in the Deposit Account has now doubled. If we had moved that money into either the Business or Personal Accounts, we would have found something to spend it on. Instead, we have "seed money" for our third month.

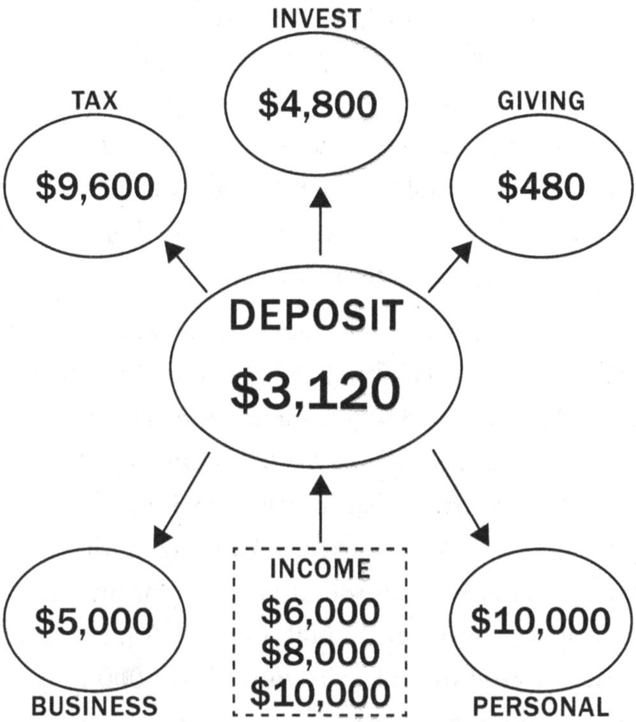

Month Three

In this scenario, there have been no sales to feed the Deposit Account early in this month. That's just a reality of business. There will be months when your income is zero or a very small amount. When this happens, decisions have to be made about how to live on less personally or reduce business expenses.

It is at this moment that bad decisions tend to be made. Most people tend to start cutting things that are important but not urgent for their businesses. I don't want you to do that. If an expense is important to your business's ability to generate income, the stability of your mindset, or your personal growth, it should never be cut. You may save today, but it will negatively impact your results in the future. This would be similar to cutting down a money tree that, over time, produces to harvest what it has on it today. In most circumstances, it would not be the right financial decision. You may even create a roller coaster cycle of living rich, then living poor. That's no fun for anyone.

So, here we are in Month Three with no money coming in yet. We need to find a total of $15,000, to cover $5,000 for our Business Account and $10,000 for us personally. Fortunately, we have our "seed money" that we left in our Deposit Account to start. We apportion that to cover any immediate bills in our Business and Personal Accounts, bringing that account to zero. I like to work in round numbers for my examples, so let's say we transferred $3,000 from the Deposit Account. So now, we need to find an additional $12,000 to carry us through the month.

In Chapter 18, "The Money Wheel," I'll show you several ways to find the money you need to fund your accounts when the deposits are not coming in. For this example, we're going to borrow the money from our Investment Account and maybe even our Tax Account. To borrow means we will need to repay them. We are self-financing our deficit. Document that the Business and Personal accounts owe IOUs to the Investment and Tax accounts. We *will* repay that money in the same manner as if we had borrowed it from a bank or charged it to a credit card. The upside of borrowing from yourself is that there is no interest. Now, if this continues every month, you must re-evaluate your spending.

For this month, there's no need to move percentages into the Tax ($9,600), Invest ($4,800), or Giving Accounts ($480). Remember, they only get funded when money is coming into the Deposit Account. It's easy to be tempted to fall back on your old ways here. This is when your financial muscles are strengthened and your ability to overcome temptation begins.

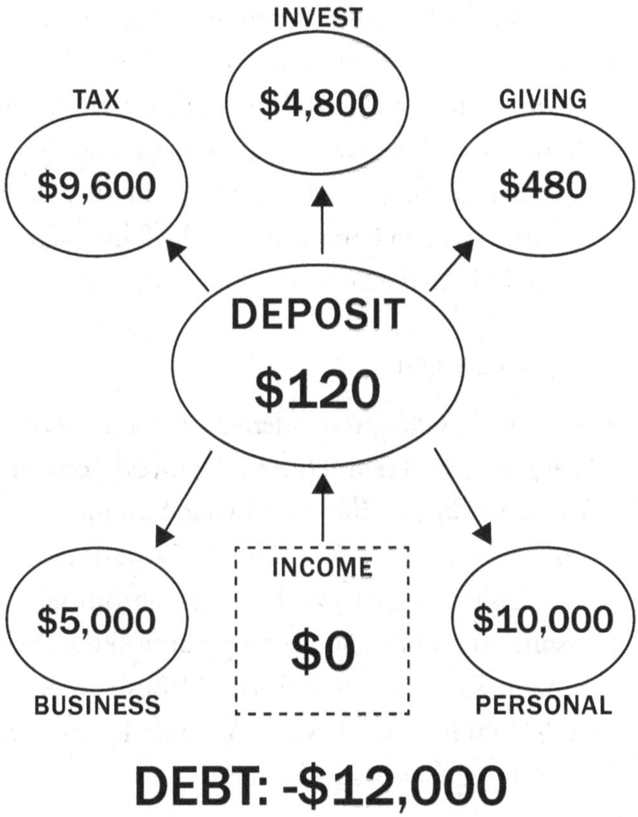

Month Four

Let's assume this month looks exactly like Months One and Two.

First deposit = $6,000

- 20 percent ($1,200) gets transferred into the Tax Account.
- 10 percent ($600) transfers into the Invest Account.
- 1 percent ($60) goes into the Giving Account.

  This leaves us with $4,140 in your Deposit Account. We will split this between the Business and Personal Accounts, leaving a small amount in the Deposit Account. So, $2,000 transfers to each of those accounts, leaving $140 in the Deposit Account for now.

Second deposit = $8,000

- 20 percent ($1,600) gets transferred into the Tax Account.
- 10 percent ($800) transfers into the Invest Account.
- 1 percent ($80) goes into the Giving Account.

  This leaves us with $5,660 in the Deposit Account. We're going to split this between the Business and Personal Accounts again, leaving a little in the Deposit Account. So, $2,000 transfers to the Business Account and $3,000 into my Personal Account, leaving a total of $660 in the Deposit Account.

Third deposit = $10,000

- 20 percent ($2,000) gets transferred into the Tax Account.

- 10 percent ($1,000) transfers into the Invest Account.
- 1 percent ($100) goes into the Giving Account.

  This leaves us with $7,560 in the Deposit Account. At this point, the Business Account only needs an additional $1,000 to achieve my budget. So that's all we move from this check to that account. The Personal Account only needs another $5,000, so we will move that as well. By managing the money from the Deposit Account, we now have the following:

- Tax Account = $4,800
- Invest Account = $2,400
- Giving Account = $240
- Business Account = $5,000
- Personal Account = $10,000
- Deposit Account = $1,560

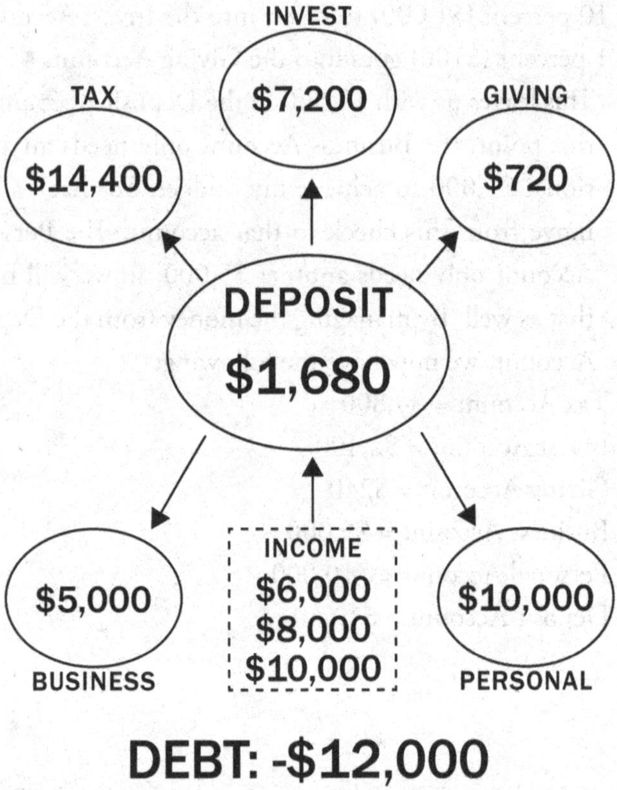

The only difference from previous months is that we are going to use the remaining monies in the Deposit Account to pay toward our IOUs. We will do this each month until the debt is paid. What's important is to maintain the plan by transferring funds into each account before using any of the remainder to repay the borrowed funds. Consistency with the plan makes all the difference in how well it works for you.

If this is a struggle, then your expenses are way too high. The reality is that you are living on a budget that exceeds what the business can support. At the end of a full year, if you have operated in a monetary zone between neutral and negative, you've got to cut expenses.

You are building your own Wealth Pyramid by taking the steps in this book. And one thing you cannot do is spend everything you earn if you want to be successful in achieving wealth. In the next chapter, I will show you how to take control of the money that goes out of your business.

CHAPTER 15

Expenses

IT IS VITAL to take control of the money that flows out of our businesses. This includes understanding our expenses, how we think about them, and how we organize them. It's relatively difficult to make money and ridiculously easy to spend it. Gaining control over spending is non-negotiable if you intend to achieve wealth. Thinking of ways to lower expenses needs to become a habit. It may seem tedious at first, but once it becomes a habit, it can be quite inspiring. Coming up with a new way to spend less becomes as much fun as learning a new way to generate more income.

When we live according to Parkinson's Law (work expands to fill the available time), an increase in income incentivizes us to expand our expenses proportionally. The more money we make, the more money we spend. I'm not sure why we all seem to think this is normal. It's something I want you to become aware of and learn to fight. By using the Wealth Machine, "spending" our money is no longer the default.

In this chapter, we will work on making "spending less" the default pattern of our thinking and actions.

We all have plans for our future money, right? We hear others talk about it and we do it ourselves. We say, "When I'm making X amount of dollars, I'm going to do this." It's like we are waiting for the dollars to show up from some outside source. If you're like most people, you already have some of those dollars readily available, but you're missing an opportunity to have them work for you.

When you came up with your definition of wealth in Chapter 2, I'm pretty sure you didn't include "having high expenses" as part of it. Wealth is not only about the amount of money you have or how much you spend. I see wealth as freedom. Anything that slows my progress toward my financial goals, delays my path to freedom, and I feel handcuffed. Once I discovered the key to unlocking those handcuffs, everything changed for the better; My wealth journey accelerated. Now, the key wasn't a quick fix. I don't ever expect to find a get-rich-quick scheme. I'm willing to work for what I want. It's so satisfying to see my wealth grow through my efforts. And that's what I wish for you, too.

Get Perspectives from Outside Your Business

When we desire different results, we need to change our process. It can be challenging to determine exactly how to go about doing things differently. I decided to start by lowering my expenses. I asked myself, "What could I cut without hurting my business?" Here's what I decided:

At the beginning of each year, as it was nearing time to prepare the information for my tax accountant, I would take all of my expenses from the previous year and ask five people whom I trust, who understood my business and my vision, to take a look at them. They didn't have to be accountants or even good with numbers, but they needed to understand who I am and what I was trying to achieve.

My challenge to them was this: "You *must* cut 12.5 percent off the total budget. What are you going to cut?" I used 12.5 percent for a specific reason. By giving that specific number instead of 10 percent or 15 percent, I let them know I had a particular amount of money I wanted to eliminate from my expenses. It made them feel like they were in the CFO seat with me, and it was time to crush a major task!

Amazingly, these five people came back with different answers. Their answers were all good and true from their perspective. This is so important to understand. While I definitely wanted answers to come from different perspectives, I had to keep in mind who was giving me this advice. Were they as motivated as I am to grow my business? Did they have a plan or idea that delivered a higher-than-expected return for their business? If they didn't, their suggestions might have been to cut spending in an area I knew to be vital to my business. And that's okay. I asked for input, not directives. I wanted unique suggestions to consider for my business plan to evaluate from my perspective after they presented their ideas.

Next, I considered each answer and its potential impact on my business in the coming year. Now, if I implemented all those cuts, it would result in a reduction of around 35 percent in expenses. I wasn't totally out of control with spending on my business, so a cut that drastic would probably have made a negative impact. However, those differing ideas increased my awareness of what I might change. As expenses in those areas changed throughout the year, I was better able to make judgment calls on what actions to take. Their ideas helped me innovate new ways to adjust my business spending.

While I highly recommend doing an exercise like this for your business, I'd much rather have you learn to track your expenses in the present moment to avoid the need to reduce them at the end of the year. Why not do it as you go instead of discovering how much more you might have saved at the end of the year?

Tracking Your Expenses

Few entrepreneurs know how to track and organize expenses early in their businesses. As mentioned earlier, the primary focus is typically on how to make money, not the expenses of the business. And tracking expenses isn't sexy. It just isn't as appealing as earning more.

At the end of each month, gather your bank statements, credit card statements, and any receipts you have from cash expenditures or even a personal card for a business expense. While I don't recommend mixing business and personal expenses, sometimes it happens. Once, while traveling for business, I left my business credit card at the office. All I had with me were personal cards, so I had to use those. You might make a purchase at an office supply store, and while you're there, pick up some markers or poster boards for your kid's school project. It happens. That's why we want to save our receipts, so we can sort everything at the end of each month.

During your end-of-month review, I want you to list every expense on a spreadsheet. You're not going to do anything strategic with the information yet, just get it into a single document. Why do I want you to do this? You may be thinking there has to be an easier way, and I'm sure there is. The purpose of creating the spreadsheet manually is to ensure you are confident in your ability to understand it. I don't advise delegating this very important work until you know how to do it yourself.

Add each month's information to the same spreadsheet. You're going to have to do this for your taxes anyway. I'll warn you, if you don't document your expenses correctly, you'll end up paying more taxes. I can guarantee you that paying more taxes than you need to will NOT help you on your journey.

Adding the information to the spreadsheet each month, while those expenses are fresh in your mind, will shorten the amount of time necessary for tax preparation later. Before I started doing this monthly, I was spending forty-plus hours during January and February of each year preparing for the tax forms that were due in March. Those were hours I could have invested in earning more money instead. I also lost the vast ability to analyze where I was each month and make adjustments, which is a critical part of being a CFO. Hey, I never claimed to be a great CFO when I first started. Like you are doing now, I read books, interviewed people, and learned from my mistakes.

Adding your expenses to the spreadsheet monthly also allows you to catch where you might be losing money or what bills you are struggling to pay. This gives you the opportunity to run your business better. Let's compare this to driving a car. What happens if you never look at the gas gauge? You don't know you're low on gas until a light comes on the dashboard or you hear a warning sound. Then, you start looking for the closest station. If you had been watching the gauge all along, you would have known of the potential issue sooner and been able to seek out the most economical solution, a station with the lowest gas prices. Instead, you are mentally kicking yourself as you watch the dollar amount at the pump climb.

As your business grows, it may be beneficial to utilize an app that tracks your expenses or hire someone to do this for you. However, it's crucial that you do the work first. This will increase your understanding of where your money is going and the expenses necessary to run a business efficiently.

After tracking expenses for a few months, you'll begin to see how some can be grouped together. Once I began this process, I found there were five primary groups of expenses in my real estate business.

1. **Education.** I attend many educational events. Expenses related to them include tickets, tuition, and travel expenses such as airfare, hotels, and meals. If you are an entrepreneur or independent contractor, I highly recommend having an expense category that reflects education. This would include any classes you take in

person, non-fiction books you purchase to be mentored by great authors, and fees for coaching that you receive. Investing in your education is the wisest move and best financial investment for your business.

In January of 2018, I was exposed to Tony Robbins's training. I love his work. I love his determination to find ways to blow through every brick wall he encounters. At that time, he offered several levels of classes to grow both personally and professionally in any realm of business. When presented with multiple levels of opportunities, I'm the kind of guy who wants to go straight to the top. I signed up for his Business Mastery conference to the tune of $10,000. The program was in West Palm Beach, Florida. That is not an inexpensive city to spend time in. My travel expenses alone were another $5,000. You know it's not going to be cheap when, on the walk between the hotel and the conference center, you pass a McLaren dealership (one of the most expensive luxury cars in the world). If you're not sure what that is, do a Google search for images and the retail cost of McLaren vehicles.

When others around me learned of this, they thought I was nuts, that I was wasting my money. I was told this was a stupid idea. I was told I should have invested my money in other things. They reminded me that this was "a lot" of money to spend. Period. Not just a lot to spend on an educational event. They weren't wrong. But I understood that they were giving me that advice from *their* perspective. Their comments were based on what they would or would not do with $15,000. I attended that event determined to gain knowledge that would bring me more than what I spent. I went there with the attitude that it would be a life-changing event. And was it ever! I learned so much at that event. I benefited both personally and professionally. To this day, I will tell you it was the most valuable conference I have ever attended. I anticipate relying on the knowledge gained there for the rest of my life. Never underestimate the value of the right education.

2. **Listings.** As a real estate agent, there were specific expenses related to acquiring and managing property listings. By grouping these expenses together, I could see exactly what it cost me to run that aspect of my business well. By analyzing this grouping, I got a better idea of what expenses provided the most value and which didn't. Consider the activities in your business that generate the primary income and group them together.
3. **Buy Back Time.** In the beginning of our businesses, we have to exchange time for money. Then, for our businesses to grow beyond what we can reasonably do ourselves, we must figure out how and where to spend money to gain some of our time back. If we don't do that, we limit how much our businesses can grow because we just can't make more time. Another risk of not figuring out how to reclaim some of our time is burnout, where we have nothing left to give to our businesses or our relationships. No one wants that.

4. **Generating Leads.** I invested heavily in my ability to create referrals for my business. To do this, I needed to have consistent contact with my clients. Any system or service I purchased for this was considered an essential expense.
5. **Technology.** Now, this has as many positives as it does negatives. Yes, technology can help accelerate your business in many ways. It can make you more efficient. It can systematize services. It can also change fast, requiring constant updates and increased expenses. The cost of constant change could ultimately be a negative, slowing productivity. For example, a real estate team adopted a sophisticated new Customer Relationship Management (CRM) system, promising automation and efficiency intending to provide better service. However, after implementation, the team found the system unintuitive and poorly integrated with their existing tools. Team members spent hours learning the new software, troubleshooting glitches, and adjusting workflows. Instead of saving time, productivity dropped for weeks, agents grew frustrated, and some reverted to manual tracking methods to stay on top of leads. What was meant to be an upgraded time-saving investment became a bottleneck. I like to apply the concept of KISS to my tech: Keep It Simple Stupid.

The Budget as a Tool

I think it's sad that so many people I've encountered think of having a budget as tying their hands. It's as if the budget itself is a mean old dictator limiting their fun. If that's your mindset around having a budget, it's time to change. The budget is not the boss. It is nothing more than a tool you use to dictate how your money moves in your best interest. If you've ever done any gardening, does your shovel dictate where your soil goes? No. The shovel is nothing more than a tool. *You* use it to place the soil where it will do your garden the most good.

With the right mindset, using a budget can actually be freeing because you can make conscious decisions about where your money goes, why it goes there, and the benefits it's providing. So, I beg you to embrace the budget as your best financial tool in relation to your income goals. The budget is meant to support your income goal. The great news is that you are the one creating it!

When I first started my business, my expenses were running at approximately 20 percent of my income. As my income grew, so did my expenses. I would adjust my budget accordingly. That was until I realized that my budget had grown to 40 percent of my income. That was just unacceptable to me. I started asking myself this question: "How can I operate on less and still make more?" While that seems obvious as the ultimate goal, it's not an easy question to answer. Yet, when you have your spreadsheet of expenses and a trusted group of outsiders reviewing the details, it becomes much easier to come up with answers. The focus shifts to what is really needed to achieve your income goal.

In my case, my income goal was $500,000 per year as a real estate agent. If my average commission check was $10,000, that meant I had to serve fifty clients. Playing with the math, I assumed a fifty-fifty split with half buyers and half sellers. Going back to my spreadsheet, I broke down the costs associated with each type of client. If my expenses for working listings were higher than those related to sellers, I could slide the numbers in my budget in their favor. If the costs involved in working with buyers were higher than the income those transactions provided, I might consider pivoting and working with more sellers.

By tracking my expenses and comparing them to my income, it became apparent where my time and money would be best invested. If I hadn't been tracking my expenses, I might never have realized this and spent too much time taking actions that weren't helping me earn more money. Tracking reveals where there might be either shortcuts or booby traps on your path to wealth. It will help you streamline your financials and the timeline it takes to achieve your goals.

Another critical question to ask each time you add to your spreadsheet is this: "What expenses do I no longer need?" Look for long-term expenses that may have been beneficial when you agreed to them but might not be serving your needs today or in the future. Look closely at short-term costs that may have been part of an experiment to see if they added value. If they don't, end them as quickly as possible. Learn the lesson and move on quickly.

What's important here is that I'm not asking you to run through your expenses with a pair of virtual scissors and start slashing away. I'm asking you to *find* whatever amount adds up to 12.5 percent of your current expenses. If today is the day you are comfortable making those cuts, great. If not, remember that the goal is to make that much in cuts over the next thirty, sixty, or ninety days. No matter when you make the cuts, remember that your business operations budget has changed, and update your Wealth Machine accordingly.

CHAPTER 16

Taxes

LET ME BEGIN this chapter by stating that I am not a tax professional. The advice I share here is based on my experiences and those of my clients. If you are deeply indebted to the government with back taxes, I highly recommend consulting with professionals in this field. They may be able to help you develop a specific plan for paying back taxes. That being said, let's consider some strategies for avoiding this tax issue.

Have you ever been behind in paying taxes? Or has tax time come around, and what you owed was more than you had readily accessible for payment? I have never been in that situation. Even when I was on welfare, I always paid my taxes. So, I can only guess what it feels like to owe the government money. The closest I get to this feeling is when I talk with my clients. I can see how it destroys their lives, how they don't sleep at night, how they feel they have to hide it from the government and maybe even their spouse if they don't already know the situation.

I remember that gnawing pit in my stomach when other debts were owed and I didn't have the money to pay them. I don't know why it seems to affect the gut, but that feeling is awful. There are steps we can take to avoid that feeling when it comes to taxes. Those steps lead to having the right amount of money available at the time they are due.

If you are generating income while living and working in the United States (or even as a US citizen living outside the US), the 16th Amendment to our Constitution allows the federal government to collect income taxes from any source, including wages, interest, dividends, and rental income. It is a duty placed on all of us who have taxable income to pay a portion to the government. Whether you agree with how much you pay or how the government spends that money is irrelevant to this chapter. No one likes to talk about taxes. No one I've met so far has "being behind on paying taxes" as part of their wealth vision. For that reason alone, let's set the premise that to be truly wealthy, we cannot fall behind on paying our taxes. The goal of this chapter is to show you how to get caught up on your taxes and never get behind again.

The subject of taxes always comes up with my clients. What I often hear from those who are behind in paying taxes is this: "Austin, I just don't have enough money to pay my taxes." What they're actually saying is, "I spent all my money." Or "I don't have a system in place for taking out the government's share when I get money." The good news is that I do have a system for this. It is one of the key elements of the Wealth Machine.

Eliminating the Problem

Over 50 percent of the entrepreneurs I work with tell me they are behind on paying their taxes. That tells me that whatever system or process they are using is not working. The hardest part when coaching is getting clients to admit they need help. It's just like someone with a compulsive addiction. The first step to getting better is admitting they need help. When they don't, they choose to let their habits control the situation. They are unwilling to change.

When my clients agree to change their current system or process, the first thing we do is build their Wealth Machine. I have them set up the separate accounts we covered in Chapter 13. Then, they look up their previous year's tax forms or contact the person who did their taxes to determine the tax rate they owed based on their reported income. Do you see an additional problem when not filing your taxes? Without this information, you are unaware of the primary cost of doing business, and you lack the data to set yourself up for success.

The next step is to commit to transferring that percentage from their deposit account to their tax account whenever funds are deposited. By doing so, the excuse "I just don't have the money" the next time taxes are due is eliminated.

You might wonder how this is going to fix the problem of being behind on taxes. It doesn't. I don't worry about that at first. My initial goal is to establish a system to eliminate the possibility of getting into this problem again in the future. It is all about creating new financial habits.

When You Owe Back Taxes

If you are behind paying taxes because you spent the money that should have been set aside, you may wonder where that additional money will come from. I'm here to tell you that you don't have a choice. This is an obligation like any other debt. If you don't pay your mortgage, do you get to keep your house? Not likely. What if you stop paying for your car? You'll soon find it being repossessed.

If you get far enough behind on your taxes, you risk even more. You risk having fines added to what you owe. Get far enough behind or owe a large enough amount, and you risk going to jail. How will you generate income then?

So, where does the money come from to pay back taxes? Like it or not, it will need to come from your Personal Operations account. It will come from clawing your way out of financial mismanagement. All the extra money you now have from properly managing your finances will help reduce this debt. You might even take it from your Invest account to start. I mean, can you see yourself having stocks or rentals only for the government to tap into those assets to be paid back? That doesn't make sense. I want you to do both: chip away at your debt and continue to invest in your future. The "both" part is great for your emotional stability during this situation.

Failing to take care of taxes as you receive income will ultimately result in more work and sacrifices on the back end, negatively impacting the money you have for your family. You will have to live on less. You will need to tighten your spending, possibly even skipping a vacation or two, to come up with the money.

With some clients, I recommend that they round up the percentage of money they move into their Tax Account to use toward paying those back taxes. The end result is the same, though; there's less money to move into the Business and Personal Ops Accounts, thus requiring a of tightening up of spending. The hard reality is that if you owe taxes and you don't have the money to pay them, you probably don't deserve to live the lifestyle you have chosen. It is time to step back into your actual reality. This can be hard mentally and emotionally but resolving the situation will allow you to ultimately accelerate your wealth plan.

If You Are Caught Up

If you do not owe back taxes, if you are already using a system to set aside tax money on a consistent basis, congratulations! My question to you is this: Can you make your system better? Can you get more accurate with the exact percentage you need to pay? Can you achieve the goal of having exactly the amount you owe in taxes, no more, no less?

Many people get excited when they receive a tax refund. Not me. A tax refund is not "free money." Receiving a refund means I overpaid the government. In essence, I gave them a zero percent loan. That money was not available to me to invest or otherwise use to enhance my business or personal life.

If you regularly receive a refund on your taxes, I want you to do some simple math. Let's say you earned $200,000 and you paid estimated taxes of $50,000 or 25 percent. When you filed your taxes, if you received a refund of $10,000, consider adjusting the percentage going into your Tax Account to 20 percent instead. Then, you will have access to that extra 5 percent of your income to fund your Business Account, your Personal Account, or even to increase the percentage you set aside to invest. The rate you need to set aside for taxes will not likely be set in stone, and it's unlikely to be a round number. It will flex as your income changes each year. Commit to doing the math or getting the actual percentage owed from your tax accountant every year at tax time and make adjustments accordingly. This will help you make informed decisions for the right reasons throughout the calendar year.

Lowering Your Tax Liability

One of my mentors shared a story about attending a training event on vision and goals. One of the first questions asked by the instructor was, "Who here wants to pay more taxes?" Quite a few hands went up, mostly by people who had attended this event before. The rest of the audience was confused. Why would anyone want to pay more taxes? The instructor's answer was this: "We should all want to pay more in taxes because when you owe more, it's because you earned more." Paying more in dollars is okay. Paying a higher *percentage* of our income in taxes is what we want to avoid. It's your tax liability we want to focus on.

Believe it or not, I paid a higher percentage of my income toward taxes when I earned less than I do now. Now, I implement some simple strategies for my business operations expenses that allow me to pay a lower percentage today.

- Tracking expenses. I can guarantee that most business owners give away more money in taxes than necessary because they're not organized with their expenses. They don't know what or how much they can write off when tax season comes. Tracking expenses is the first place to find free money for your business.
- Hiring a CPA. When I did my own taxes, I saved money by not paying a fee to a CPA. However, after hiring one, it quickly became apparent I had been losing money by overpaying taxes. I didn't have the knowledge required to do it as well as they could. The US tax system is extremely complex. According to Public Law 117-154 (06/23/2022), the U.S. Tax Code is 6,871 pages as of this writing. When you include the federal tax regulations and the official tax guidance, the number of pages rises to approximately 75,000, which makes it almost impossible for the average reader to finish in less than six months.

  Don't you think it's a better use of time to hire someone who works with tax information every day than to try to figure it out on your own? Once I started working with a CPA, the money they saved me in taxes far outweighed any fees they charged. And their fees are tax-deductible, so it's a double win to work with a tax professional.
- Understanding deductions and credits available to you. There are more expenses you *can* deduct from the taxable business income than not. Some of the most common

places you may be making contributions for your future that can benefit your tax obligations are: 1) Contributions to your Individual Retirement Account (IRA), 2) Simplified Employee Pension (SEP), 3) Health Savings Account (HSA), and 4) any 529 accounts where you are saving to help your children with college expenses.

- Owning rental real estate. This is a vehicle I have personally taken advantage of to increase my wealth and reduce my tax liability. I won't go into the details of this, as the explanation could fill another book. I will tell you, though, that the success I've had with this strategy has contributed significantly to my personal wealth plan. Talk with your CPA about the specific advantages before deciding to own a piece of rental income yourself.

Establishing your Tax Account and becoming disciplined enough to set aside the proper percentage into it will make a huge difference in both your ability to stay current with the amount of taxes you owe and in your peace of mind when it comes to tax debt. Implementing any of the other strategies in this chapter is icing on the cake toward minimizing your tax liability.

CHAPTER 17

Income

TO THIS POINT in the book, we've been getting a handle on our spending. Now, let's get to the more fun aspect of wealth: your income. When I ask people how they feel about their income, most will tell me it's not enough. They want more. In our society, we've been taught that more is better. More will allow us to live more lavish lifestyles, give more to charities or loved ones, and experience a sense of peace or well-being.

In my experience, unfortunately, most people are not taught that managing their money can have a greater impact on their wealth than earning it. Once the strategies we covered around spending have been implemented, there will be more funds available for your wealth plan. But maybe that's not enough for you. In this chapter, we will explore how we think about earning money.

The Big Question: Time vs. Money

I had my best year in real estate in 2016. I closed eighty-eight homes while working an average of 38.5 hours a week. I knew in my heart that if I did good quality work, I could accomplish the same result as others in less time. By tracking everything, I was able to lower my business expenses. By being highly organized, I could serve my clients at a higher level. Other agents closed as many transactions, but it took twice as long. I was 100 percent committed to working smarter, not harder, and it paid off.

Fast forward to 2017. I set a goal of innovating and optimizing my working hours so that I could earn the amount I wanted while working just twenty hours a week. One of the most time-consuming parts of being in real estate is the time spent with people who want you to sell their home. You make an appointment to go to their home. You drive there. You do a walk-around to determine its condition. You give a presentation about the service you provide and then form a hiring and representation agreement. Even if it's only a thirty-minute drive from my office, the time required for listing appointments adds up fast. I determined that it was likely I'd spend two hours at the property and then have a thirty-minute drive home. This doesn't consider the possibility of the client being late, canceling, having their kids at home causing interruptions, or a dog that is a major distraction—all variables that need to be considered when managing your daily work as a real estate agent.

I wondered if I could hire someone else to drive to the home and do the walk-through to verify information about the property, and then have the homeowners come meet me at my office for my presentation. The value of the hours saved would be greater than the cost of hiring someone to do the legwork. Do you see how I think? I want to reserve my most valuable work for myself and am willing to pay others to do the rest.

Sure, I could have innovated *and* worked more hours to achieve an even greater income, but I value my time more than my money. Don't get me wrong. I truly believe if you want to get somewhere, you have to work your butt off. However, I also believe it is vital to do the most important things in the shortest amount of time possible, in the most efficient manner.

Before we get into strategies for increasing your income, I want to ask you two very important questions:

1. How much time are you willing to exchange for money?
2. How much money are you willing to exchange for time?

These two questions were part of Chapter 15 on expenses. Let's dive deeper into them. To increase your income, you might be able to work more hours. For salaried people, this might involve having a side gig. Or you can do more potent work, work that has greater value to those who pay you to do it.

If you are currently an employee and your plan is to do better work to earn more money, why aren't you doing that already? If you are already able to provide greater value and haven't presented that to your employer, they may become suspicious when you bring it to their attention. They might think you've been holding back, and that becomes a trust issue, which can backfire on you.

If, instead, you propose to your employer that you have a desire to move up within the organization and work together to lay out a plan for that, you're more likely to succeed. They might support you in earning certifications or other education that will bring greater value to the business and then offer higher pay for your new knowledge and abilities. An increase in potency will likely require additional education or a change in how you think about your work. That will require time and effort. It's easier to commit to working more hours. However, time is limited. No one wants to work *all the time*. It's just not healthy for your mind or body.

If you are a business owner, working more hours can be challenging because you might already be maxed out on the amount of time you can give. Why does this happen so often? Well, I'll remind you again of Parkinson's Law; work will expand to fill the amount of time you give it. When I meet with clients, I often hear, "Austin, I want to do more. I just don't have any more time to do it." My answer is this: "Well, you don't have more time because you're giving your current work way too much time."

This comment always throws them sideways at first. That's because it's an entirely different line of thinking. They are thinking one way, which provides one set of results, and I think completely differently. Now the question is this: Will they be open-minded and hear me out?

Sometimes, we don't think a whole lot about the number of hours we're working because "it's how much I need to work to get the job done." What I have found both personally and for my clients is that when you lessen the number of hours you allow yourself to work for your business, you'll find ways to get the same amount of work done in fewer hours. Practice putting a cap on the amount of time you allow yourself for specific tasks and see what happens. You will either come up with better ways to get the work done, or you will focus more intently on it and work faster.

Now to address question two. This directly reflects what we covered in Chapter 15 on expenses. There are places where you could invest some of your money to gain back time.

- Hire an assistant. Find someone with the skills to replace twenty or more hours a week of your time. A good test of whether it would be of value to hire an assistant is to list out the tasks you complete in a single week and how long each takes to complete. Then, go back through the list and put a dollar value on each task based on your average hourly income. Anything that amounts to less than half your hourly rate is worth considering delegating to someone else.
- Make an investment in technology (software or an app) that allows you to streamline your systems and processes.

When you regain time, put those hours back into your business, focusing on the highest-quality tasks that no one else can do. In this way, you stop working *in* your business and have time to work *on* your business. This is when you can create or seek out opportunities to generate even greater income.

Understand Your Hourly Rate

I want you to think about this in the opposite way that most people do. I want you to decide how many hours you are willing to work to earn the income you desire. Most of my clients find this challenging because they initially focus on the amount of income they want to generate and then on the number of hours they think it will take to do so.

To begin, I highly recommend that you determine how much you earn for an hour of your time. Divide your gross income by two thousand. That's the number of hours per year most salaried people work (forty hours a week multiplied by fifty working weeks in a year). I like round numbers, and I like to think we all can take, at a minimum, two weeks of vacation or personal time every year.

We are not going to get too mathematically complicated. Let's think about these things in general terms. If you are an entrepreneur or a contract worker, I hope you keep track of your hours. I think you'd have to for billing purposes. Your math might be simple because you charge by the hour and have a set hourly rate. Whatever your situation, I want you to determine what you are paid in gross in exchange for an hour of your time. Again, keep it general. Don't start subtracting taxes or business expenses. Just get a round number we can work with. Here's an example: Income goal $100,000, divided by 2,000 average hours worked per year, equals a $50 hourly rate.

How to Earn More

To increase your income, you're going to want to increase that hourly rate. Before you can do that, you'll need to increase the number of services you provide. If you're unable to do that, this whole idea could create a new set of issues for your business. Be aware that increased service may increase your business expenses. All this needs to be taken into consideration. The good news is that you are the CFO and the one making this decision.

I once met Brendan Burchard, a coach with several billionaires as clients. I asked him how he got them to pay him, and keep paying him, for his coaching. His answer was to give them more than what they are paying for. This was a simple answer, and one I could put into practice immediately.

List out in detail what you *are* paid to do. If you're a salaried employee, this might be your job description. If you're a business owner, it's the list of services you provide to your clients. I understand that you may provide a certain number of services to one client and another group of services to another. Just list them all out. Review them and think about how you might enhance any one of them.

One of the ways I've succeeded in this is by increasing my communication with clients. Clients who hire you will expect a certain standard of service. Go above and beyond "standard" by communicating more often. By doing this, you demonstrate your accessibility to your clients, which has tremendous value. I always want to be the one calling my clients with updates. If they call first, asking me for an update, I see that as a ding in the level of service I'm providing. Now, the more you communicate, the fewer people you will have time to communicate with. In return, you'll need to charge a higher fee to reflect the higher level of service you're now providing. At first, it might be scary, but overall, it will be worth it.

I was fortunate to be exposed to personality assessments at a fairly young age. They helped me to understand my own personality and how I communicate. They also helped me to recognize the personality traits of others and how they communicate. It's almost like being able to speak another language. When I can communicate with clients in a manner that best suits their personalities, I provide value in a way they are most likely to recognize.

Another method of increasing value is being a rock they can cling to in a storm. Most clients will hire you when they are facing problems, right? Otherwise, they just won't need you. You are hired to solve problems. They may be feeling a variety of emotions related to the problem. The problem might be causing financial issues. Your third-party view of their problems allows you to seek solutions without emotional attachment. When you can give clients advice that works for them from their perspective, not what works from your perspective, they'll come to trust you and want more from you.

Mo Money Mo Problems

Now, when you start earning a greater income, understand that some stress usually accompanies it. Like it says in the song by Notorious B.I.G., "Mo Money Mo Problems." We've all been raised to chase the money. Just know that doing so comes at a risk.

Previously, I shared how I ended up in the hospital due to stress. I learned the difference between bad stress, which is caused by urgency and other people's demands, and good stress, which, for me, comes from having opportunities to create more business. The common denominator, though, is that it's all stress. Striving for more money can quickly create more problems.

I don't want you ever to have an experience like I had. I want you to find a healthy balance between the amount of time you are willing to give and the amount of money you desire. If you don't get this right, all the other equations used to attain a work/life balance will equal little more than a bunch of useless lessons.

PART FOUR

CHAPTER 18

The Money Wheel

BEFORE WE GET started on this building block, I want to ensure that you understand that these last six modules are designed to help hold everything together. Assuming you have completed all the recommended work to this point, you have a solid foundation with the Cheviron Wealth Pyramid, using the personal building blocks. You have increased your awareness of how you handle money and made some changes already. You have reviewed your spending and created your debt and net worth sheets. You are using the Wealth Tracker and probably even the Wealth Machine to improve your cash flow management.

In this chapter, we'll cover one more tool to add to your financial arsenal, the Money Wheel. It's a simple resource to help you find cash when you need it. I refer to it anytime I face an opportunity or challenge that requires more money than I have readily available. It helps to build a bridge between the time I need the money and when my investments gain the needed growth.

My money wheel looks like this:

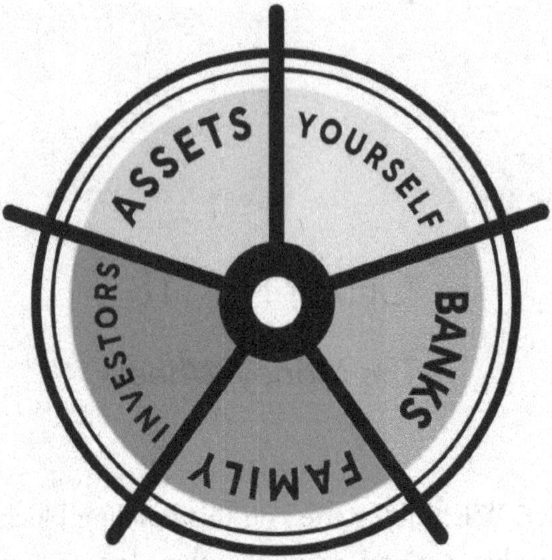

I strongly advise you to think through your available sources of money and create your own money wheel. Yours might look a bit different from mine, but I'm confident we have some sources in common. Let's go over them.

1. **Ourselves**. As I covered in Chapter 12, I have many mentors. There's one I spend time with in the Canadian woods every year. We get dropped off in the wilderness for about a week. It's a great time to unplug, think, recharge, and get some good fishing in. I was talking with him about how I needed money for a particular project. When I explained where I was considering getting the money, he gave me some of the best advice I'd ever heard. He said, "When I need money, I like to borrow from myself first."

At this point in my life, I had never thought about borrowing from myself. My first thought was always to borrow from a bank. Per my mentor's advice, I added myself to the Money Wheel first. Now, rather than automatically borrowing, I consider whether I should change where my own money is invested. Is it a better move to cash out an asset for my new project, or is there a way I can borrow from myself?

2. **Banks.** This source includes every institution you have used to cover costs of anything from a mortgage to a car. It also includes the bank where you have deposit accounts. If you have been a loyal customer, you are more likely to have this as an option. One of my mentors told me this: "Get your money ready before you need it." This is great advice!

   I hope this never happens to you, but if you ever need to borrow money in an emergency, understand that getting a loan takes time. The bank will always ask what you need the money for and review your credit score. It's part of their risk assessment. By establishing a relationship with a banker when you don't need money, getting it when you do need it will be easier, and they may even be willing to fast-track the time frame.

3. **Family.** Now, this may or may not be feasible. I don't know your family situation. For all I know, you could be the person family members come to when they need financial help. If you do have family members you can

ask, treat their loan the same as any other. Put it in writing. Commit to a pay-back schedule—as short a term as possible. And it is best if you can keep it private. The rest of the family doesn't need to know your business unless the loan is for a business they are a part of. In my case, family members are always rooting for me, for my success. They are happy to be part of my growth toward wealth. I hope that's the same for you.

4. **Private investors.** These are people who have available cash and are always looking for opportunities to invest. You might find a private investor at a networking event. They may be someone who is already in your personal contact list. Or someone in your contact list might refer you to another interested party. There are investment groups in most cities. Connect with them and become educated about their interests.
5. **Assets.** Remember the list of assets created in the Wealth Tracker from Chapter 5? As you do regular reviews of that document, pay attention to their worth. Decide which you will sell first if a need arises. Keep that in the back of your mind.

Invest a little time thinking about each source and how much money you might have access to within each. As you get better at managing your money, living on less, and even increasing your income, know that the value of each space on your money wheel will change. The limits you have today should not be the same as your limits in two, five, or ten years. Also, consider what other sources you might add to your money wheel.

There could be many. I've only covered a handful here, as I have found them to be the most common among my clients.

When and How to Use the Money Wheel

In this section, I'll give you some examples of the benefits of using the Money Wheel to create forward progress in your wealth plan. Let's say you have money coming in. You are managing it wisely, funding all your accounts, not keeping much in cash. By using all of the funds from your Invest Account, you go from being cash-rich to cash-poor but asset-rich. That's how the system should feel and work.

When another opportunity or challenge arises before you refill your Invest Account, utilize the Money Wheel to find the amount you need. Let's go through a few scenarios.

> *Scenario 1:* Let's say an emergency occurs, such as your dog or cat needing life-saving surgery. Unless you have pet insurance, you may need to pay for it upfront or make a substantial deposit on the total amount. If that is not in your budget because you invest nearly all of your cash, where is that money going to come from?
>
> Getting money from yourself is not an option. You could get a small loan from a bank. I'll tell you now that the bank is unlikely to lend you money for this situation. You may have to offer them something else as collateral against a loan.
>
> You could apply for a new credit card or request a limit increase on an existing one. Even though it's quick to apply, it can take time to actually get the card. And a downside of

getting a new card is the interest rate that will be charged if you can't pay it off quickly. If you have more money coming in soon but don't have it yet, that might be an option, as long as there will be enough to pay it off after funding your other accounts.

You might ask a family member for a temporary loan as a bridge between now and your next income deposit. Keep in mind their feelings about pets. Rather than considering pets as family members, they may view them as expendable and suggest putting them down instead. This is where it's important to know your audience. Know who might sympathize with your situation and who may not. If they don't have the money accessible, or they just don't believe it's something they want to do, don't let your emotions about the situation rule the day and cause a rift you'll both regret later.

In my case, I have private lenders on my list, but I don't know of one who would lend me money for my pet emergency. They're interested in larger investments with a solid anticipated return.

Next on the Money Wheel are my assets. If the expense is small enough that you know you can recover from it within a couple of months, I don't suggest selling an asset to get the money. It might be a last resort option. I'd much prefer to leverage one temporarily, such as borrowing from a line of credit on a property, if no other source is readily available.

As you can see, I've worked my way around my Money Wheel and thought through the best options to get the money needed.

Scenario 2: In this scenario, you need a much larger amount of money. Maybe your car needs a new transmission, and the repair will take a week or more. So, you need a rental while the car is in the shop. Starting at the top of the Money Wheel, let's assume you are short of the necessary cash. You want to avoid using a credit card because of the high interest rates. A bank loan might be a viable option at a much lower interest rate. A family member might be an option. Again, if they're rooting for you and have the cash available, this could be an easy fix. Since this money is not being used for an investment, private lenders would be out. It may also be possible to leverage an asset for the required amount.

Scenario 3: Let's step up our example and assume you have an incredible opportunity to purchase a real estate property for $250,000. You need $50,000 for the down payment. Your investment account doesn't have that much in it because you keep that money working for you. The bank isn't likely to loan you $50,000 since they're also looking at providing the mortgage on the property. Unless you have wealthy family members, it's not likely you'll get it from them.

Since this purchase is an investment in an asset, private investors may be the best option. They would likely set the loan at a slightly higher rate than the bank charges, but it would give you the opportunity to bridge the gap. Even if that seems to be a good answer, continue circling your Money Wheel and consider your assets. Do you already have equity in your home or an investment property?

Would it be possible to get a home equity line of credit for that $50,000? If you have stock assets, are you able to leverage them? Or are there assets you could sell to get the money? You might have to weigh your options. Is the value of owning an asset you already have greater than the value of owning this new asset?

There's tremendous value in creating your own money wheel. Use it as a guide to walk through all financial options available when the need or opportunity arises.

When You Get Your Money Right

What happens when you get your money right? Let me share a story about how I helped one of my clients, Joyce. When I was selling real estate full-time, I helped Joyce with the purchase of her home. It is important to recognize that homes are personal for people. It's within those walls that they feel safe and create memories. As an agent, I understood that and worked to view each property through the eyes of my clients. With most, I became friends. Some preferred to keep our relationship transactional, and that was okay, too.

About ten years after purchasing this home, Joyce called me to say she was not doing well. By this time, she was in her seventies and had been diagnosed with dementia. She felt it was time to move to Florida to be near her son. She wanted to sell her home. Since I helped her purchase this home, I knew a lot about it. We arranged a meeting with Joyce, her son, me, and my uncle, who was close to Joyce and had been helping her a great deal.

The home had always been well-maintained, so it was in great shape. I told her what I thought the fair market value was and offered to buy it myself. I said, "Joyce, this will be the smoothest transaction you've ever had, and when it's finished, you can live here as long as you need. Making this move to Florida may take some time, maybe even several months, and that's okay with me. When you move, take whatever you want and just leave the rest. I'll take care of anything left behind. You don't need to worry about having the house empty. You won't be bothered by the process of having strangers walk through your house, like you would if you listed it for sale." Joyce was thrilled with this offer, and we agreed on the details.

I'm not sharing this story to prove to you that I'm a nice guy. This story demonstrates what you can do when you take care of your money. I was in a position to help Joyce and her family, and in the end, I also helped my own family. As a real estate agent and investor, I never want to let a good property get away.

The key point of this story is that when I made that offer to Joyce, I didn't know exactly where I was going to get the money to purchase it. I just knew I could. The value of the property was $150,000, and I needed a 20 percent down payment plus closing costs. I rarely keep a lot of my money in cash. It's always invested. It's always working for me. So, I had to decide where and how to move my invested funds to collect this money.

Here were some of my options:

- Sell some stock
- Ask a family member
- Seek a private investor

- Sell another asset
- Use a credit line

I ended up combining money from a private investor with some from a line of credit I had on another property. It took Joyce about two months to make her move to Florida. I paid to have the house cleaned out. Now, I had two options. I could sell it or keep it in my portfolio as a rental. I was only able to do this because I had handled my money correctly. Because of my efforts, I was able to help someone I cared about during a hard time in her life. This is a perfect demonstration of wealth to me.

CHAPTER 19

Insurance

I REMEMBER HEARING this advice, but don't recall where it came from: "As you're climbing up the mountain, throw some dirt back in the valley in case you fall." Based on my own experience, I would change that last phrase from "in case you fall" to "when you fall." When you take new actions to achieve greater wealth, you are bound to take a few tumbles. The important thing is to be prepared to handle the fallout from those tumbles.

We protect ourselves from the personal and professional challenges we will face through insurance. Like taxes, insurance is not a sexy topic unless you're an insurance agent and it's the foundation of your livelihood, or you have good insurance, and you are expecting a large payout.

Going back to tossing dirt behind you as you climb, the purpose of insurance is to provide you with a soft landing *when* you fall. When I asked people if they were over- or under-insured, more than half said they were "probably under-insured." Knowing you are underinsured is one thing. Having "probably" as part of the answer bothers me more. It means you have not given insurance its proper value or attention.

No one wants to learn any life lessons the hard way. When you delve into it, insurance is a very simple tool to protect you, your loved ones, and your assets. It only gets hard when you fight paying for it. I've had more people than I care to list tell me they didn't have money for insurance. I always come back to them with this: "It's not that you don't have the money for it. It's that you haven't placed enough value on having it." In my opinion, insurance should be a priority in your budget, alongside food. It's that important.

Having a pantry or freezer with a week's worth of food may not seem like a big deal if you live in a town where there's a grocery store every mile or so. For some, it may seem like too much. But when you're too sick to leave your house or, in the case of people who live where it snows, if you *can't* leave your home due to the weather, that week's worth of food has tremendous value. Insurance is just like that.

Too many people I know learned the value of having insurance the hard way. As a real estate agent, you are an independent contractor, and most of the companies you associate with do not provide health insurance. Over the years, I've heard story after story of agents facing health challenges that have cost them nearly everything they owned because they had no health insurance. A few I've known ended up filing for bankruptcy due to medical debt and had to start over on their path to wealth. Some never did. They never recovered from that experience.

In my experience, had I not had health insurance when I spent those eight hours in the emergency room, I would have had a $60,000 medical debt. With insurance, my share was only $5,000. While $5,000 is a significant amount, it is more manageable than $60,000. Time in the ER is never planned or expected.

Other challenges can also create unplanned expenses and stress. For example, one of my rental properties was set on fire. Fortunately, I had insurance on the property. My deductible was $5,000. This was a manageable amount for me. In this case, however, a crime investigation was underway, and the insurance company wanted to wait until it was resolved before paying me for the damage. That investigation took an entire year. However, as we covered in Chapter 18 on where to find money, I was able to get a loan to cover the time gap.

I restored the property to good condition, and it began generating income relatively quickly. When the insurance check arrived, I was able to pay off the "gap" or "bridge" loan. The lesson I learned through that experience was that if I had better insurance, I would have received a much larger settlement check. I hadn't done that because it would have cost me more each month, resulting in a greater out-of-pocket expense than I would have liked.

A friend of mine had a lot of damage to her fence and landscape when a wind shear went through her neighborhood. They rushed to put up a temporary fix that night on the downed fence because all the neighbors had dogs that needed to be kept in their yards. This involved relocating some large tree branches, installing braces, and replacing boards. The insurance agent who assisted with the claim said the payout might have been a bit more if they had taken photos *before* moving tree limbs or fixing the fence. The homeowner's sense of urgency to re-establish "normal" overrode their thought process around filing a claim and likely cost them money.

What's the moral of these stories? It's this: Just because you have insurance doesn't mean you understand how insurance works. I strongly suggest scheduling a time with your insurance agent and showing up with a list of potential scenarios. Ask, "What happens if…?" Have your agent explain the process when claims are filed, including time frames and the detailed information the insurance company will want. You may discover it's in your best interest to upgrade your coverage.

Protecting What You Have

The very first asset most of us own is a car. And that's likely the first time we learn about the need for and cost of insurance. When you bought your first car, did you know there were three main aspects of insurance? It is not likely, unless one of your parents is an insurance agent and you actually listen when they talk about it.

Here are the three main aspects to consider when purchasing car insurance:

1. Personal liability and property damage: This covers damage you cause to persons and property of others, up to a certain point.

2. Full coverage: This is a step above. With full coverage, you and your vehicle are covered as well as any damage you may cause others.
3. Gap: If you have a loan on a vehicle, this may be a good idea to investigate. If your vehicle is totaled, full coverage may only pay you the vehicle's value at the time of the accident. If you owe more than the value of the vehicle, Gap insurance would provide the balance needed to pay off the loan.

What's important here is to talk with your insurance agent about your specific situation and get the coverage that brings you the best protection for your needs.

When it comes to our homes, if we have a mortgage, we are required by the bank to have insurance on the property. It's fairly standardized based on the size, type, and quality of the physical premises, unless you live in a geographic area with greater than average risk for weather-related damage, such as hurricane, earthquakes, or flooding. Other things that may be taken into consideration are swimming pools, playground equipment, or trampolines. While they are sources of great fun most of the time, they also create potential risks for injury. If you have any of those, it might be wise to add what's called an Umbrella Liability Policy to your budget. This will pay up to a specific dollar amount if someone else gets hurt on your property and sues.

Homeowners insurance is designed not only to cover damage to your property but to replace the contents of your home, especially in the case of fire or flood. How do you let the insurance company know what was in the property? Most agents will recommend that you walk around your home recording every corner, every closet, cupboard, drawer, and storage bin. If this seems like a lot, it's probably because you have a lot of stuff. Anything you would want to replace in case of a fire will need to be documented.

When working with your insurance agent, be sure to ask about any additional riders that might be helpful or even necessary to protect your belongings beyond the basic homeowner's coverage. An insurance rider is an add-on feature that can be included in an insurance policy to expand or customize coverage. Think of it as an upgrade or optional feature you can attach to a basic policy. It may cover items such as jewelry, art, guns, coins, or antiques.

If you are renting an apartment or other property, it's advisable and often required to have renters' insurance. This will cover the cost of replacing your belongings in the event that they are damaged or lost at the property. An example of this might be a fire in an adjacent apartment. There may be no physical damage to your apartment, but your belongings could have smoke damage or even water damage from the fire department's efforts to put the fire out.

Going back to how to pay for all the insurance you need, be aware that most insurance companies offer discounts for what they call bundling. This means that you get more than one type of insurance from the same company, such as car and home insurance. If you currently have different types of policies with other companies, it's well worth your time to ask each for an estimate if you bundle your policies.

Your Health and Your Life

The next area I want to cover is health insurance. If you are working for a business that provides it, consider yourself lucky. Without health insurance, you are one decision away, yours or someone else's, from a catastrophic failure of your financial future. Health plans vary tremendously. You will want the help of a qualified professional to assist you in determining the best type of plan for you and possibly your family.

Health insurance is like taxes. You really don't want to have too much or too little. Having too little means you possibly will have to pay for that gap later. Having too much means, you might miss an opportunity to fund your future at a faster pace. Find the right balance.

The most important insurance to have does not protect you but protects your loved ones. It's life insurance. The last thing most of us want to think about is "What happens when I die?" When you're young, this seems like such an unrealistic situation that you don't give it much thought. That's pretty normal. I believe that part of being a responsible adult is to financially take care of our loved ones, especially when we are no longer around to do it in person. At the time of this writing, most insurance experts recommend getting a life insurance policy for ten times your earnings. So, if your income is $75,000, you would want to have at least a $750,000 policy. The idea behind this is to enable your loved ones to continue living the same lifestyle that your income provides. Or they could use the funds to pay off any debts left behind.

Just imagine the impact on your family if they were to lose your income. What if, upon your death, they could pay off the mortgage and car loans? Wouldn't that relieve a tremendous burden? Not having you there would, of course, continue to be painful, but having financial worries on top of it would be worse. Life insurance will help alleviate at least some of those financial woes.

If a large policy is simply out of the question and beyond your current budget, at the very least, get a policy to cover funeral expenses. I happen to believe that we should cover expenses related to our remains. Someone else should not be expected to cover that expense. As a starting point, call a local funeral home and obtain a rough estimate of the expense. Get a life insurance policy to cover that amount. Then, work your way up to having a policy that will replace your income ten times over. There is something to be said about being a responsible adult and taking care of your responsibilities yourself.

The Deep Dive

Pull out the information on every insurance policy you currently have. I would like you to determine whether you are over- or underinsured. Review the deductibles for each policy. The lower the deductible, the higher the policy's cost. Consider how much you could reasonably afford in the event of a car accident or some property damage. If that number is higher than your current deductible, get a new quote from your agent. By increasing your deductible, you may save enough on one policy to cover the cost of another you haven't yet purchased.

Here's something to think about: If you have a $500 deductible on your homeowner's insurance and you have damage that will run you $700 to repair, are you likely to file a claim? I don't think so. It's probably not worth the hassle, and the more claims you file, the more your premiums can go up. It's not worth the risk. If that's the case, why not consider increasing your deductible to $1,000 or $1,500, which you might feel comfortable handling out of pocket? This would lower your premium and allow you to use the difference for a new or better policy to cover something else.

The primary reason for having insurance is to mitigate financial risks against unforeseen adversities. Consider it an investment.

CHAPTER 20

Assets

OUR ASSETS ARE meant to help us achieve our financial vision for our lives. It requires meticulous organization and analysis of how we manage our finances to determine the assets that will work best for us.

This chapter is where we go over how to use the 10 percent of your income set aside in the Invest Account from the Wealth Machine. The idea here is to invest in assets that add to your overall wealth. Over time, the goal is to build a portfolio of assets that can replace your income or even generate more than you earn when you are exchanging your time for money. Managing income-generating assets will take time, too, but not nearly as much time as you are currently giving to your job.

Eventually, when you choose to no longer work as an employee or a business owner, your job will become managing your assets to make them continue to work and grow for you.

Managing your assets may pay you more than you're currently earning in your career. You will become your own Warren Buffett, who, as I write this book, is one of the wealthiest people in the world. You may, or may not, have the same number of zeroes in your net worth as Warren Buffett, but do the same type of work. Speaking of Warren Buffett, a bit of advice he offers is to "invest in what you know and expand your circle of competence." You expand your "circle of competence" by continuing to learn and grow as an investor through others who know more than you do.

Two Main Types of Assets

While attending a mastermind group held by one of my coaches, I had a great conversation with a financial guy. He explained to me the difference between "and" assets and "or" assets. "Or" assets are things you exchanged your money to own. These might be things like jewelry, art, clothing, or even a smaller item like a backpack. You either have the asset *or* you have your money. Most of the "stuff" we have in life are "or" assets. The "and" assets are things you can own *and* leverage to get money. This includes real estate. You can own it, live in it, and get a home equity line of credit against it to own something else.

Another example of an "and" asset would be your stock or brokerage account. There is a good chance the institution you use will allow you to borrow against your assets held by them. The reason for this is that they hold the assets and use them as collateral to ensure repayment. Now, what this means in both scenarios is that they will only loan you a portion of what the assets are worth.

Let's use your home, for example. A typical math formula for this type of borrowing is this:

Appraisal Value x Loan to Value Ratio (LTV) - Mortgage = Loanable HELOC Amount

For something like a stock or brokerage account, I typically see companies allowing borrowers to leverage 50 to 70 percent of the total portfolio value.

While you might, at some time, consider selling your "or" assets, I want you to fight to avoid selling your "and" assets if possible. It would be like cutting down a money tree that provides for you each month. Overall, that usually is just a bad plan and could put a dent in your wealth plan. The only time to consider cashing out an asset is if a new opportunity will provide a much more lucrative return than the current asset.

Asset Categories

What you invest your money in will depend on how much you have set aside. If you have $5,000, you won't likely be able to purchase rental property. You could put the money into an IRA. You might do some research and purchase a hot stock with that amount. Alternatively, you might consider investing in cryptocurrency (crypto). Those are just a few examples of how to utilize that amount of money.

What if you have your heart set on owning a rental property? You may have to leave that $5,000 sitting in your Invest

Account until you have enough for a deposit on a rental property. When you keep a rental occupied, it can start paying you immediately and continue over the long term. Additionally, the property is likely to keep appreciating while someone else is paying the mortgage. Now, you have equity in the property, meaning you owe less than it is worth. Equity is the portion of the property's value that you truly own. It is what's yours, not the banks. With enough equity, you may be able to get a credit line to borrow that equity. You could use that money to upgrade the property to charge more rent or purchase an additional asset.

On my personal wealth journey, I chose to keep buying more rentals. I would use the monthly income plus a line of credit to continue adding to my family's real estate portfolio. I chose not to spend the passive income from the rentals but invest that money back into my wealth journey instead! Those decisions made for a great investment.

Diversification

One of the most important lessons when it comes to assets is diversification. You never want to have only one category of asset. I think we've all heard the advice about not putting all your eggs in one basket. The trick is to arrange your financial life such that if any investment has a bad result, it is not personally financially catastrophic. My advice here is to go back to your net worth sheet. Take a look at all the assets listed. Do the math to determine what percentage their value is of the whole. If a large percentage is in one category, consider making your next investment in a different category.

Personally, when I started investing, I was a 70/20/10 percentage guy. I invested 70 percent in real estate, 20 percent in stocks, and 10 percent in cash. That was my general formula until I started investing a percentage in my business. It worked well for me.

Until I heard Steve Forbes, chairman and editor-in-chief of *Forbes Media* and a respected authority on finance and economics, speak at a Tony Robbins event, I didn't fully understand cryptocurrency. Known for his sharp insights and clear explanations of complex financial topics, Forbes helped demystify crypto for me in a powerful way. Steve's advice was to put 5 percent of your investments into crypto, even if you didn't understand it. If you do understand it and are studying it, invest 10 percent. I trusted Steve's expertise on the matter and adjusted my investments to allocate 5 percent less into real estate and use that money for crypto investing.

When we hear advice like Steve's, we must understand our risk tolerance. If the unknown is too scary or if the potential downside is more than we can handle, it's time to pause and get more educated about the opportunity. This ties nicely back to Warren Buffett's advice to invest in what you know.

Full disclosure: I am not a financial advisor. I'm just sharing my experience. Because I managed my money well, I have sufficient funds and a diverse investment portfolio, which mitigated the risk. Additionally, I listened and learned from experts in their field. These were not spur-of-the-moment decisions but well-informed investments. You must educate yourself about these things and decide if investing in them is right for you. Alternatively, consult with a financial advisor to make informed decisions and achieve your wealth plan effectively.

Use the Wealth Tracker to determine if you are on track or if you need to make adjustments, such as diversifying or rebalancing your portfolio. Due to the volatility of some investments, I recommend reviewing your assets every six to twelve months at a minimum.

Remember, the goal is to acquire assets you want to hold for the long term, not make daily changes. That's too risky. Be patient. We do not want to gamble with our assets.

There are several asset buckets I use for the money in my Invest Account:

- Real estate
- Stocks, bonds, and commodities
- Crypto
- Cash

My current mix of assets looks like this:

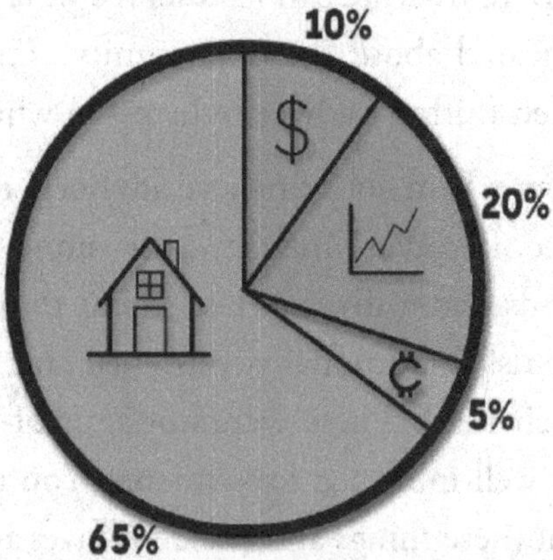

If these categories make sense to you, the next step is to determine what percentage of your net worth *you* want to have in each. What do you take into consideration when rebalancing your assets? Do the math to determine the value of each category to ensure you are still hitting your percentage goals.

Let's say my goal is to have 65 percent in real estate, 20 percent in stocks, 10 percent in cash, and 5 percent in crypto. If one or more of my stocks increases tremendously in value, that might throw off my percentages. It may be wise for me to sell some of the stock and allocate the cash to whichever category is lacking. If the value of my crypto leaps, it may be time to cash out some of it and hold the money for another real estate opportunity. Doing the math. Making these decisions is the "job" I mentioned you'll need to do once your wealth plan has been achieved.

Having been involved in real estate for much of my life, either through my dad or my career as an agent, I chose to have a higher percentage of my net worth there because it's something I understand well. If the value of my real estate increases so that it's a much larger percentage of my total net worth, it's time for me to reallocate some of its value elsewhere. This might mean selling a property and investing the revenue from the sale in stocks, crypto, or maybe just holding it in cash for another opportunity.

Perhaps your experience might guide you to invest in businesses rather than stocks. There are plenty of people who do this. Some individuals invest in a business as a silent partner, holding a percentage of ownership. Others may invest and contribute to a business's success as consultants or advisors, helping the business grow. When it grows large enough, they sell their interest to the other owners or participate in the sale of the entire company, gaining their share of the profit from the sale.

The key element here is to determine what you know or learn about what interests you and then follow those paths to assets that fit into your wealth plan. Then, continue to analyze the value of your assets and potentially rebalance them. Balancing your assets is a way to prepare to withstand storms that may negatively impact one category or another. It's almost like buying insurance to prevent catastrophic loss.

CHAPTER 21

Passive Income

IF YOU DECIDED to walk away from your job today, how much money would you have to live on? How long would it last based on the monthly cost of your current lifestyle? If you have done the work in the earlier chapters, these answers will come easily to you. You will know what your "island money" dollar amount is. You will also know your current budget. If you can't answer those questions, it's time to go back and do the work. A quote from *The Richest Man in Babylon* says it all: "The work shall set you free." That's what this entire book is about. The work you put into managing, thinking, and organizing your financials is what will set you free and move you forward on your journey to true wealth.

If your current financial situation cannot support your lifestyle for as long as you are likely to live, it's time to develop some strategies around passive income. Passive income is income one earns without putting a lot of direct energy, effort, and time into it. Hence, it's passive. This is the goal of achieving wealth, isn't it? To be able to have freedom of time because you have freedom of money.

I like to think of passive income the same way I think about insurance. You buy insurance policies to cover you in case of a catastrophe. In the case of passive income, you want to create enough of it to cover your expenses in the event you are no longer able to work, or you need to slow down. When I had my health episode, not only was I grateful to have health insurance to cover the bulk of my medical expenses, I was also grateful for the passive income streams I had, as they covered my monthly budget while I was forced to come up with a Plan B for how I was going to live my life.

Having the ability to earn income is a wonderful thing. Being able to earn passive income is even better because we don't have to work as hard for it. It allows us to reclaim our time while still generating money into our Deposit Accounts. This is the ultimate goal of everyone seeking time freedom. For some, the goal is to have enough passive income to retire. They may even be willing to work for forty years or more to achieve it. For others, the goal is to stop working or switch to part-time work much sooner by generating passive income now. Which is it for you? Have you given much thought to creating passive income? What do you have to lean on if you are told you can't work for ninety days?

The topic of passive income has become important for some of my clients due to the season of life they're in. Maybe they're nearing retirement and are unhappy with the amount they've saved. They're seeking other options for incoming funds to cover their budget, so they don't have to make drastic lifestyle changes in retirement. For others, they may be working way more than forty hours per week to earn enough to support their lifestyle, and they're tired of missing out on fun events with loved ones. They don't want to work the hours anymore, but *do* want to keep the lifestyle.

When I began investigating options for generating passive income, it was as if a whole new world opened to me. I didn't just want to create one stream of passive income. With a single stream, there's always a chance it could dry up. I wanted to create several. My initial goal was to generate $1,000 a month through passive income. That was a number that was worth my attention. From there, my ultimate goal was to have my passive income meet or exceed my monthly expenses. Learning about the different streams of passive income was next.

Passive Income Methods

While there are hundreds of ways to generate passive income, learning about all of them, since I won't be investing in all of them, would probably be a waste of time. Initially, learning about a few options to choose from is a better strategy. Once you have one stream that brings in your first dollar amount goal, then move on to investigating another. As of the time of this writing, I personally have six streams of passive income, and I spend way less time monitoring them than I ever spent working in my primary career.

You are welcome to do a Google search for ways to generate passive income. In this chapter, I will cover my experiences with setting up and growing my streams.

1. Dividend Income. I used the money from my Invest Account to purchase stock. Some of the stocks I bought produce dividend income. Money earned through dividends or capital gains on investments is generally considered passive income. I didn't take any action to earn it. The stock earned it. The dividends have been reinvested in more stock.
2. Sales Referrals. This is when I receive a referral from one of my clients for a friend or relative, and I then refer that person to another agent. When the agent helps them buy or sell a home, they give me a referral fee for sending them the lead. There are many fields in which this type of income can be generated, not just real estate. When you are well-connected and have proven trustworthy, it becomes easy to make arrangements with other professionals in which you receive a fee in return for sending them new clients.

   Another approach is to get involved with affiliate marketing. This is where you recommend products and services in exchange for a percentage of sales made by the company that sells them. In some instances, you do not even have to purchase the product or ship it yourself. You simply drive leads to the company that does. This is what most social media influencers do.
3. Real Estate Rentals. Having rentals and managing rentals are two separate things. When you own rentals, they generate passive income in that collecting rent and paying mortgages takes very little time and effort. Managing rentals is a different story. The work of find-

ing good renters and maintaining properties can be quite time-consuming. The desire I have with my rentals is to only collect passive income. I hired a property manager to handle the rest.

If owning and managing rentals isn't in your plans but you believe in the value of investing in real estate, you might want to consider Real Estate Investment Trusts (REIT). REITs are companies that buy, operate, or finance income-generating real estate. Do the research to determine if this is a good opportunity for you.

4. Owned Business. For me and most of my clients, owning and operating a business requires our direct involvement. When you can grow your business and put a team in place to carry out the day-to-day operations necessary to keep it running, the amount you take out of the business can become passive.

   There are also business opportunities where you can "set it and forget it," requiring very little of your time after initial creation. These include digital products, such as those sold on Etsy, online courses, books or other publications, mobile apps, audiobook narration, and spreadsheet creation. Many of these so-called "side hustles" have turned into powerful passive income generators for thousands.

5. Interest. This is another way you might use the money from your Invest Account. Consider loaning it out to others and charging interest on the loan. The interest is passive income. If you choose to do this, invest some

time learning how to document the loan properly, including a repayment schedule. In the event of a loan default, it is essential to have proper documentation to use in court for resolution. The risk associated with your initial investment is higher here than with other forms of passive income. Please consult with a financial advisor to truly understand the risk associated with all types of investments.

6. Assets. The great American entrepreneur, Jim Rohn, said, "Kids should have two bicycles, one to ride and one to rent." Think about how you can generate passive income with your existing assets. What do you own that you could rent? With the advent of companies like Turo, hundreds of thousands of people have rented a second or third vehicle that would otherwise be rarely used. Others have converted unused bedrooms into Airbnb rentals. What are *your* opportunities?

The whole point of generating passive income is to keep you afloat and provide peace of mind if and when your career undergoes a significant change. It's a great way to prepare for a slowdown into retirement as well, no matter your age. Additionally, it's a great way to eliminate having all your financial eggs in one basket.

CHAPTER 22

Inheritance

YOU HAVE WORKED hard on the many aspects of the Cheviron Wealth Pyramid to achieve your definition of success. You have identified how you think about money and why. You have achieved a high awareness of where your money is coming from and where it is going. You have pared down your expenses. You have worked on building multiple streams of income. The next step in your wealth journey is to decide what happens to your wealth after you're gone.

It's important to address this question today because no one is guaranteed tomorrow. The goal is not to be rolling over in our graves, upset with how our heirs handle what we have worked so hard to attain. Depending on your relationship with your legal heirs, you may want to specify exclusions to access to your cash, stocks and bonds, real estate, jewelry, art, antiques, family heirlooms, and retirement plans for those you don't want to have access to them. We've all seen Hollywood's dramatizations of inheritance situations where the dog, cat, or maid gets everything, and the family receives nothing. What's your situation, and how do you want it to go down? Decide and meet with an attorney to get it all in writing, just the way you want it.

The first question to ask yourself is this: Do I want to leave anything when I am gone? Or do I plan to spend it all before I go? If you want to leave something behind for the next generation, how do you picture it will affect those who receive it? What is your goal for how your wealth journey will impact others?

I've been documenting my wealth journey for my children, and perhaps their children. I want them to take all the steps you and I have taken thus far in this book, so they too can achieve wealth. Hopefully, they'll never experience being on welfare and can start their journeys farther along the path. The results of my efforts will prime the pump, so to speak, of their wealth journeys.

As I've mentioned several times, a significant portion of my wealth journey has been, and will likely continue to be, the accumulation of rental properties. I plan to teach my methods for choosing good properties and getting the money to purchase them to both of my kids. If I'm seventy-five when I pass on, my kids will be in their fifties. Will they even need or want to inherit what I've built? Or will they have achieved their definition of wealth by then?

A friend of mine gave me a book titled *Die With Zero: Getting All You Can from Your Money and Your Life* by Bill Perkins. It's a common-sense guide to living rich, rather than dying rich. It made me think about the purpose of my wealth plan in the long run.

What if, rather than holding off until I pass to share my wealth, I decide to give each child one of my properties when they turn eighteen or twenty-one? How does that impact the rest of their lives? Me being me, I would include a stipulation that they could either live in it or receive the rental income from it, but not sell it. How does that change the trajectory of their lives? And does handing off the rental income of two properties really impact my life much when I intend to own fifty properties by the time my kids are that age?

Can you imagine being twenty-one and owning a home free and clear, without having a mortgage on your personal residence ever? What could you do with the money that would otherwise have gone to the bank so you could have a roof over your head? Think about the kind of start you could give your kids on their wealth journey.

I was discussing life with one of my mentors, and he told me he believes it is his responsibility to give his kids the best start in life that he can. We were discussing college and whether the parents should pay for it. He said, "Absolutely, yes!" If I took his same attitude toward giving them a home, then my answer would be "Hell, yes!"

I have heard others talk about telling their kids, "You are my responsibility until either age eighteen or twenty-one, then you are on your own." Whatever you decide is what you decide. I hope you consider the options closely and make the best decision for yourself and your family. Lend them this book and talk about the steps you are taking on your wealth journey.

Your wealth journey doesn't end with the achievement of your definition of wealth, unless your definition also includes the distribution of that wealth after you're gone.

Questions to Consider

There are many questions to consider regarding what happens to your accumulated wealth when you no longer need it. Here are just a few:

- Who do you want to have what's left when you are gone? Loved ones? One or more charities? Your community?
- What do you want to be known for?
- Who gets what items and why?
- Who doesn't get anything, or receives very little, and why?
- Is there something it would be wise to give before you pass on? If so, what, to whom, and when?

One of the many reasons we compile all our financial information is to have it readily available when creating a will, trust, and power of attorney, ensuring our accumulated wealth is handled in the way we want. You've generated all your assets. Now it's time to take care of them and give them a place called "home" after you are gone. Having the proper paperwork in place is a responsibility related to your wealth plan, just like any other paperwork. How do you pay for these legal documents? With money from your Invest Account.

After living through the aftermath of my mom's untimely death, I can tell you that death can tear families apart. When my mother passed, I was responsible for going through her personal belongings and deciding where they went. Remember, I was only seventeen at the time. I had no clue as to the value of anything she had or who she might want to have it. It was *not* a good experience. Do you want to leave your family members in this position? By making the choices now for how you want your assets handled, you can eliminate unnecessary additional grief to your loved ones when you're gone.

Lessons to Leave Behind

How do you teach someone how to handle an inheritance? This will most likely be a spouse or significant other, and possibly your children. Obviously, you believe you're doing a good thing by providing something of value to them after you are gone. The question is this: Are you setting them up for success with what you leave behind, or are you setting them up for failure?

In my example, a large portion of my wealth is invested in rental real estate properties. It's vital my wife knows where they are, how much income they provide, and how they are handled in case I pass before her. She may want to let things ride and continue to enjoy the revenue they generate. Or she may not be as comfortable owning real estate as I am and choose to sell them, or even a portion of them. Either way, it's part of my obligation to her to discuss her options and whom to trust to help her when she has questions after I'm gone. Introducing her to the team of professionals I use to handle the rental properties is essential.

I learned this lesson from one of my clients. She and her husband owned two rental properties. She didn't want anything to do with them. Her husband handled all the details about those properties.

When he passed, she didn't know anything other than there were two. She didn't even know how much income they generated. She called to tell me to "just get rid of them." She told me that if I sold one of the properties, she would give away the other home for free because it had structural issues. While the repairs would be expensive, ranging from $3,000 to $8,000, this didn't make sense because it was worth so much more. Losing her husband left her grief-stricken and overwhelmed. These were valuable assets that had appreciated since their purchase, but because she was stressed and ignorant of the details, she was ready to take a loss. Would you want that for your loved ones? Probably not.

This is just one of many examples why we must teach those who will inherit our assets how to use them best and what they are worth. It is not difficult and could make all the difference to the generational wealth your family gains because of your efforts. Or it could all stop with you. Talking about death can be difficult, but it is a conversation worth having. Educating and informing your loved ones about your wishes, intentions, and assets can help prevent them from feeling overwhelmed when grieving a loss and make them less likely to make poor decisions during a difficult time. You get to choose.

So, as you think about the division of your assets, your wealth, after you're gone, also think about what advice you would give those receiving them. Let them know why you invested in them and how you would handle their liquidation if that's their choice. They may not take your advice, but at least you've provided them with food for thought on how to handle those assets for their greatest benefit.

CHAPTER 23

Giving

EARLY IN MY personal journey, I didn't recognize the importance of *giving*. I didn't see a correlation between wealth and giving. My mindset was only on generating deposits and accumulating assets. Through the guidance of mentors and my own reading about wealth, I came to realize that giving is a significant part of achieving wealth.

When I give, I not only impact the recipient or recipients, but I also set the stage for an exponential increase in giving in the future. That's because I have four little eyeballs watching when I give. Whether we like it or not, there are times when our children learn more by watching what we do than what we actively try to teach them.

I mentioned earlier in the book that we often travel as a family so that my daughter can participate in competitive cheer. During these trips, it's also important to include activities my son enjoys. We often spend time in arcades, as that's something he enjoys. On one of our trips, the hotel where we were staying had a basketball hoop but no basketball available. Fortunately, there was a store that sold basketballs next to the arcade where we planned to play. So, of course, we picked one up before hitting the arcade.

As we were leaving the arcade, my son realized he didn't have the basketball. I wasn't happy that he hadn't kept track of it, and we headed back into the arcade to find it. Within just a few seconds, we found a group of kids in the arcade with their families, and they had a basketball. I asked if they had found it in the arcade. When they said yes, I explained that it was ours and asked if we could please have it. The kid gave us the ball, and we headed out.

Before we got to the door, my son stopped me. He said, "Dad, we should give them our game cards." We had purchased three hours in the arcade and had probably an hour left on them, but it was time to head out. My son had the conscience thought, and generous spirit to consider those kids who had to give up the basketball. Since they wouldn't be entertained with the ball, he thought to give something else. Where did he learn that? Hopefully, from watching his mom and me giving freely. I can't find the words to describe the joy his actions and thoughtfulness at the arcade brought to my wife and me. We are hopeful he will continue to grow as a giver as his life progresses.

The One Percent Change

The plan is to transfer 1 percent of what goes into your Deposit Account into your Giving Account. That's where

I want you to start. When I was struggling, this gave me pause. I just didn't think I had enough to share. But then I began doing the math. If I had a $1,000 check coming in, 1 percent would be only $10. I wasn't sure that amount would help anyone, but I also didn't think it would affect my life much either. So, I started the habit of setting aside 1 percent and didn't give it much more thought. When Thanksgiving came around and I could donate enough to the local food bank to feed four families, that felt pretty good. How cool is it to provide one of the most basic human needs? I had no idea who those people were, but being able to give back to my local community in a positive way changed me.

I began looking forward to giving. I had a rather large check come in from a real estate transaction between Thanksgiving and Christmas. One percent went into the Giving Account, and when my church asked for some clothing as gifts for families in the area, my wife and I took the money from our Giving Account and went shopping. Again, with 1 percent of the incoming amount, we were able to help provide another basic human need. My awareness of my relationship with money began to change. I was becoming the person I desired to be—a better version of myself—and it wasn't hard to do.

The Next Step

Once you develop the habit of transferring 1 percent of every deposit into your Giving Account, double it. Returning to the previous example, 2 percent of a $1,000 check is $20. If I did that a few times, it would enable me to provide a Thanksgiving dinner for eight families. How cool is that?

What else can we do with our giving money? We can buy books for the local library or school. If that doesn't plant seeds for growth in the community, I don't know what does. If this book has changed the way you handle money for the better, consider buying another copy with some of the funds in your Giving Account and handing it to someone else who might benefit from it. I'm not telling you that to sell more books, but to encourage you to become an advocate for others to improve their financial futures.

Strong financial management becomes a giving game that becomes more fun the more we give. And the more we give, the more we appreciate what we keep.

With a giving mindset and habit, you will get a positive jolt each time you realize the good you can do. In my case, I quickly increased the percentage going into my Giving Account to 5 percent, then 10 percent. Now, my family is able to help fund an innovation center for kids, make a healthy donation to the advancement of cancer research, and work with local charities to provide more and better services. The satisfaction of helping others is indescribable and profoundly changes your perspective on financial wealth.

Easy to Do, Easy Not to Do

If you are in the early stages of your wealth journey, you might think that setting aside money in a Giving Account is a good idea, but you are already stretched in so many other areas that you think it's okay to put it off. "Giving" is the first account that we eliminate or neglect. If there's a shortage in what's needed to cover operations, either for a business or personally, the account that gets shortchanged is almost always the Giving Account.

The reason for this is that the Giving Account is never urgent. Taxes are urgent. Operations are urgent. Even the Invest Account could be urgent when an incredible opportunity presents itself. While giving is important, "urgent" will always trump "important" in most of our lives.

Giving is essential not for what it is but for who it helps you become. It's not so much about the dollars as the practice of giving. As your wealth grows, I challenge you to increase the percentage you add to your Giving Account. If you've exercised any of the advice in the previous chapters, lowering your expenses, tightening your budget, and managing your cash flow well, you will find it easy to increase your giving percentage from 1 percent to 2 percent. In fact, you'll barely notice the difference in the amount of money you have access to, but you will feel different as a person. You will feel more abundant.

As an ultimate goal, I'd love for you to eventually give 10 percent of every dollar earned to worthy causes. When we are entrusted with money, it's up to us to do the right things with it. When we do the right things, we become entrusted with more. I've seen this happen repeatedly with my clients. My mentors have told me stories of how an abundant and generous mindset has impacted their clients.

Scarcity versus Abundance

Remember in Chapter 2 when you considered the question, "What does wealth mean to you?" Part of my answer to that question is to be able to give freely without concern for what I have left. If there *is* a concern about what is left, that's a scarcity mindset. It's based on fear. How we think about wealth isn't dollars and cents; it's our emotions around money. The thinking is this: If I give $100 to someone who is asking for help, will it cause me to miss out on something important to me? Is this donation creating a sacrifice? A detriment?

With an abundance mindset, we know that any amount given away can be replaced. There is no sacrifice. The emotion is one of peace or gratitude for being in a position to have no fear around money. It's a beautiful thing.

To achieve a mindset of abundance, start giving your 1 percent. The positive feeling related to helping others will outweigh any fear of scarcity. As you give more often or larger amounts, the sense of abundance will grow exponentially. I love this quote by Jim Rohn: "Become a millionaire not for the million dollars, but for what it will make of you to achieve it." Achieving wealth isn't about the dollars. It's about who you become along the way.

The amount of time and effort you put into achieving wealth is an investment in future generations of your family. The lessons you learn and the practices you establish set the stage for your loved ones to do the same. When you do the best you can with what you have and make a commitment to continually understand how you feel about money, you will become increasingly motivated to learn more advanced strategies for achieving wealth.

What I found after studying my journey to wealth is that there are many parallels to the parable of the talents in the

Bible. In the story, a master entrusts three servants with varying sums of money known as "talents," each according to their ability. Two of the servants wisely invest and double the amount given to them. However, the third servant, driven by fear, buries his talent in the ground to protect it. When the master returns, he praises and rewards the first two servants, but reprimands the fearful servant, taking away what was entrusted to him and giving it to the servant who multiplied his talents.

The story embodies the importance of stewardship. When we don't use our abilities, we limit ourselves and even risk losing gains. When we step up and use what we have, we invite greater opportunities and multiply our abundance.

CONCLUSION

BY THIS POINT, you should feel more confident about the path you are on for your personal wealth journey. We began this journey by working on your personal financial situation. You have given a lot of thought to what wealth means to you. If you gain nothing else from this book, please understand that achieving wealth requires you to spend more time thinking about and managing your money than earning it.

Please understand that the definition of wealth you came up with at the beginning of this book is not carved in stone. It may have even changed after you read the last chapter. It may continue to change as you evolve and achieve greater abundance. And that's okay. In fact, it's more than okay. It means you are acknowledging your personal growth. Your vision is what helps to pull you through the mud when things get tough.

Now, you have an increased awareness of how you feel about and handle money. You have recognized how your past experiences have affected how you think about money. Consequently, you are making conscious decisions based on that awareness rather than unconsciously letting those experiences dictate how you make decisions today.

Putting in the time and effort to analyze your current spending was the most difficult part of this program. However, it should also have been the most enlightening. Remember, our money only goes where we let it. By capturing it, we can point it in a direction that takes us farther faster on our wealth journey.

The Wealth Tracker gave you a central location for your regular overview of the progression of your wealth journey. You should now know your credit score, how it impacts your wealth journey, and how to improve it. When you understand how to focus your vision, simplify your view on your current state of wealth, and categorize your spending and reduce your debt, your progress is likely to accelerate. You are better prepared to redirect what you determined to be Extras and to monitor the results of any changes on a consistent basis. When you need extra money to fund your vision, you know right where to get it.

If you're an entrepreneur, no matter the size of your endeavor, you've learned how to think like a CFO and manage the money from your business, including how to stay current with paying taxes. We even covered how to think like an entrepreneur and maximize the amount of income you generate versus the amount of time you spend working in your business. You learned about the Wealth Machine and the advantages of managing your money with it.

With the Money Wheel, covered in Chapter 18, you have opened your eyes to where you can find money to fund the various opportunities that will come your way. You understand different types of assets, the benefits of creating passive income, and the value of having insurance in case the inevitable happens.

The icing on the cake of the Wealth Pyramid is the two categories of Inheritance and Giving. This is where you look beyond yourself, beyond what you want to be, do, and have, to consider the kind of impact you can make on others. It's the endgame of true wealth.

Achieving wealth requires a vision, a system, and a guide. Everything presented here is based on my personal experience and that of my coaching clients. It has worked well for all of us, and we continue to use it as the seasons of our lives change. This book has laid the groundwork for you to develop your own wealth plan.

So, what's next? Continue to work with the tools provided here for a full twelve months. Continue to monitor your awareness and spending habits. Keep tracking every aspect of how you handle your money. By the end of the year, you should have seen a dramatic improvement in your wealth journey. You may also find yourself seeking out even more ideas and more strategies for acquiring wealth. Do it! Jump on the growth train and expand your horizons. There's no limit to how far you can go.

AUSTIN'S RECOMMENDED RESOURCES

1. *The Richest Man in Babylon* by George S. Clason

2. *You2: A High-Velocity Formula for Multiplying Your Personal Effectiveness in Quantum Leaps* by Price Pritchett

3. *Think and Grow Rich* by Napoleon Hill

4. *The Millionaire Next Door: The Surprising Secrets of America's Wealthy* by Thomas J. Stanley and William D. Danko

5. *Unshakeable: Your Financial Freedom Playbook* by Tony Robbins and Peter Mallouk

6. *Failing Forward: Turning Mistakes into Stepping Stones for Success* by John C. Maxwell

7. *The Automatic Millionaire: A Powerful One-Step Plan to Live and Finish Rich* by David Bach

8. *Die with Zero: Getting All You Can from Your Money and Your Life* by Bill Perkins

9. *Living with a Seal: 31 Days Training with the Toughest Man on the Planet* by Jesse Itzler

10. *Secrets of the Millionaire Mind: Mastering the Inner Game of Wealth* by T. Harv Eker

11. *Miracle Morning: The Not-So-Obvious Secret Guaranteed to Transform Your Life (Before 8 AM)* by Hal Elrod

12. *Getting Things Done: The Art of Stress-Free Productivity* by David Allen and James Fallows

13. *The Noticer: Sometimes, All A Person Needs Is A Little Perspective* by Andy Andrews

ACKNOWLEDGMENTS

THIS BOOK IS the result of many hands, hearts, and voices that have shaped my journey, and I am deeply grateful for each of them.

To my mother, thank you for helping me see the truth in life, even during the hardest times. If we could do it over again, we would do it differently, but we made the best of an unfortunate situation.

To my father, thank you for being the example a young man could look up to. Your guidance and character set the foundation for who I am today.

To my wife, your support has been my greatest gift. Thank you for allowing me to chase my vision, knowing that no matter what, my back was covered.

To Nate, your vision is so big that I found my place within it. Thank you for inspiring me to think beyond my mental limits.

To Grandma Clem, you were my first example of financial stewardship. Your lessons continue to guide me.

To all my financial mentors, including Jim O'Donnell, Mike McMullen, Chriss Luithly, Shawn McArdle, and many more, your wisdom and generosity shaped my understanding of true wealth. I am forever grateful for the knowledge you shared.

To Brian Buffini, Tony Robbins, and Darren Hardy, thank you for the incredible wisdom you shared when I was younger. Your lessons helped shape me into who I am today.

To Coach Scott, thank you for guiding me through the hard years of growth.

To Judy Slack, thank you for taking me under your wing and giving me the guidance and confidence to give all that I have to the world.

To my publishing team, thank you for bringing this book to life.

A huge thank you to my sister, Dr. Megan Woenker, for your invaluable insights and thoughtful feedback on this manuscript. Your keen eye and constructive suggestions helped shape this book into something even better.

To everyone whose financial decisions, both positive and negative, impacted my life, thank you. Even when we did not see eye to eye, I learned from you. Those experiences shaped me, offering lessons that fueled my growth in unexpected ways.

And above all, thank you, Jesus, for being my guiding light, always providing direction and clarity.

This book exists because of the incredible people who poured into my life.

Thank you.

ABOUT THE AUTHOR

AUSTIN CHEVIRON IS a seasoned entrepreneur, real estate expert, investor, and coach who transformed his life from collecting welfare to becoming a multimillionaire in a short period. He achieved this by developing a keen awareness of his life and purposefully managing his resources, laying the foundation for his success.

With over twenty years experience, Austin has built multiple successful businesses, developed high-performing teams, and coached thousands of entrepreneurs to long-term success. He's known for helping others clarify their life's vision and strategically align their personal and professional lives to achieve it. Austin's sustainable strategies create financial freedom, drive business growth, and promote a balanced lifestyle. He inspires individuals to grow their businesses while prioritizing family, health, and personal fulfillment.

Austin's straightforward approach, combined with his rare talent for igniting vision in others, has guided countless professionals to align their personal and financial strategies for real success. He was recognized as eXp Realty's Instructor of the Year 2021 and continues to inspire others through live training, coaching programs, speaking engagements, and online courses on the subjects of wealth, teams, and agent success.

Having summited his own mountain of success, Austin shares his lessons openly to help others navigate their unique paths with confidence. He emphasizes overlooked yet vital areas of life, ensuring his clients are "winning twice" by achieving harmony between personal vision and financial goals.

Austin lives in Fort Wayne, Indiana, with his wife, Lynsee, and their children.

Continue Your Journey with Austin

If this book has positively impacted you, are you ready to take the next step? Cheviron Coaching offers several on-demand programs and coaching opportunities to help you balance growth with your desired lifestyle because you can win twice!

Online Training Programs

- **Wealth:** If you enjoyed this book, you'll love investing over six-plus hours with Austin as he brings these concepts to life! This on-demand program dives deeper with demonstrations, visuals, and a workbook to guide you through each step. You'll gain a clearer understanding of how to apply these principles to your life and take your financial success to the next level.

- **Agent Success:** This twelve-module course equips real estate agents with the strategies to dramatically increase income while creating more time freedom. You'll master Austin's proven systems to run a thriving business without sacrificing personal priorities. Learn how to clarify your vision, systemize lead generation to build a steady stream of referrals, and maintain control over your schedule. This program empowers you to excel professionally while staying deeply connected to what matters most, lasting success and the lifestyle you've always envisioned.
- **Teams:** This six-module system helps you build and grow a team that aligns with your vision as a leader. Austin's approach focuses on teaching your team how to "fish," equipping them with the skills to achieve lasting success rather than relying on quick fixes. You'll learn to operate a low-expense model while optimizing systems that elevate your business instead of weighing it down. This program positions you to compete at a level your competition doesn't know exists!

Gain Live Proximity and Coaching

- **Cheviron LiVE:** Experience Austin's on-demand programs brought to life in a weekly group coaching call. Each session dives deep into real estate strategies, proven systems, and the true meaning of financial success, all while helping you craft the lifestyle you desire. Gain accountability, stay motivated, and connect with a community of high achievers. It's been said, "Don't say it to a Cheviron unless you mean it!" This is your chance to be in live proximity to a true guide who's been where you are and knows exactly how to show you the way.

- **One-on-One Coaching:** Reserved for leaders who've already achieved success but seek the strategic wisdom to reach new heights. These weekly personalized sessions are designed for visionaries ready to harmonize business growth with their deeper life purpose. If you're at the crossroads of scaling your success while preserving what matters most, these transformative conversations provide the clarity, accountability, and high-level strategy that only come from someone who has navigated this terrain before.

Take action now to continue building the life and business you deserve!

AustinCheviron.com